Suddenly the Sun

ELEANOR HULL

Suddenly the Sun

A BIOGRAPHY OF

SHIZUKO TAKAHASHI

PUBLISHED BY

FRIENDSHIP PRESS

NEW YORK

161036

CONTENTS

Acknowledgment

This book began with the perceptive enthusiasm of a young Baptist minister, Rev. R. Dean Short, who thought the story of Shizu Higuchi Takahashi could be enlightening to many people. He heard it vividly told by one of his parishioners, Harry S. Nako, a close friend of Shizu and her husband for many years, and brought me to hear it too.

The responsibility now was mine to try to describe a woman's journey from Orient to Occident, from feudalism to the Atomic Age, from Buddhism to Quaker Christianity. I have had help from many people.

The family of Shizu Takahashi, first and foremost, welcomed me with perfect hospitality and shared their memories of wife, mother, and sister with unmeasured generosity. To know them has been one of the great privileges of my life. They have all been named in the book, but I must add the married name of little Tami, whose memories were invaluable, and who is now Mrs. H. T. Okada. Mrs. Olive Naylor, a daughter-in-law of the Friends Pastor who welcomed and sustained Shizu, invited me to visit her in Berkeley and much enriched my understanding of the past.

The missionaries who had known and loved Shizu have entered into the project with enthusiasm. Minnie Pickett Bowles (Mrs. Gilbert Bowles) remembers Shizu's youth in keen detail, and has written me repeatedly from Hawaii, answering questions, contributing anecdotes, and blessing the effort to give more people a chance to feel the influence of her "beloved Shizuko." I was able to talk with Mr. and Mrs. H. V. Nicholson and learned much both from hearing their experiences and from feel-ing the gentleness and power of their lives. Mrs. Edith Dillon Beaman and Mrs. Alice Lewis Pearson, knowing Japanese Christian work in both countries, sent useful information. Miss Esther B. Rhoads took time from her enormously busy life as a member of the board of directors of the Friends Girls' School in Tokyo to write me several times and to secure additional information from some of Shizu's schoolmates. Mr. Sylvan E. Wallen of the Japan Committee of the Religious Society of Friends in Philadelphia has been a friendly resource man. And I am grateful to the many readers of the manuscript, not even known to me, who have supplied knowledge and experience to supplement my defi-ciencies.

My gratitude to the missionaries extends beyond those whose services I have named, to the whole pageant of imaginative and love-impelled Christian workers of all denominations who have gone overseas to share their finest treasure with new friends.

Finally, I must express my wondering admiration of the elder Takahashis, and the Nakos, and the many other Issei, whose dauntless courage in adversity, like the light of glowworms in the blackest night, has been "a thing impossible to hide."

ELEANOR HULL

Cleveland, Ohio
May, 1957

"From plum-scented veil
Of haze, suddenly rose the sun
On the mountain trail."

Suddenly the Sun

CHAPTER ONE

A Journey into the Unknown

Shizu bowed to her parents for the last time, a little stiffly, a little awkwardly, as she tried to hide her tear-filled eyes. It was a silent leave-taking, the mother returning the child's bow more quickly than usual, the father bending toward his daughter with rigid formality. Even the little sister was quiet as she watched.

Only the faint *chin-chin-chiro-rin* [1] of the cricket in its cage broke the silence of the large room. Nothing except Shizu's hastily wiped eyes betrayed the turbulent thoughts carefully hidden behind each composed face.

But inside, Shizu was crying, "Father! Do not send me to this strange place! Mother! Keep me with you! Tami, I'm sorry I teased you with the caterpillars."

The father was thinking, "I wonder if I'm really doing right in sending off my ten-year-old daughter to a Western school in the city."

The mother was lamenting to herself, "Why must this be? The time of trouble continues long."

Straightening up from his bow, the father spoke with

[1] See Glossary at end of book.

sharp emphasis. "Shizuko Higuchi, by learning well, you will honor your family name."

His words gave Shizu courage to turn around and go out of the house to the jinrikisha. Here her brother Yataro was giving directions to the blue-coated bearers who would push the baggage handcart and pull the two jinrikishas on the long journey to Tokyo.

"Ready at last, Shizuko?" Her heart skipped a beat. Yataro was always so quick and impatient. But he gave her a smile as she climbed into the jinrikisha. He motioned the handcart man to go ahead, then jumped in beside her.

"I will have to ride in my own ricksha farther on when we go over the steeper paths," said Yataro. "But I thought you'd feel less lonely if we started out together."

"That was most considerate, Niisan," Shizu murmured. He understood then! It wasn't like going back to Cherry-River Grammar School.

"We have a pleasant day for our journey," she observed politely.

The sun was shining brightly on the terraced rice fields and the pine-clad hillsides as they drew out of Chiba. It was beautiful. But Shizu felt as if a dense mist hovered just beyond the near scene, hiding all that was to come.

Mist was only water droplets, she reminded herself, and would vanish as the day went on, but in the early morning, who could penetrate its thickness?

It was 1886, and all Japan was sharing in some measure the sense of impenetrable fog that Shizu felt. Not twenty years had passed since the opening of Japan and the restoration of the Emperor to power. Japan had changed from an isolated medieval country ruled by military clans to an awakening member of the family of modern nations with the progressive Emperor Meiji firmly in control. The old fears and hostilities toward the outside world were passing. They were being re-placed by eager interest in all things Western, but it was frequently a nervous and uncomprehending interest.

"All Japanese girls must travel into the unknown," Yataro remarked, sensing her fear-laden thoughts, "when they take their wedding journey! But this trip of yours is not that final."

Shizu considered it. If it had been a wedding journey, she would be years older, and traveling into an unknown that held not only strangers, but her whole life's destiny.

On the other hand, every gift and garment, every bow and word, would be planned. Her family and friends, ancestors, and the gods, would have a part in all that happened, and even if the place and people she was go-ing to were strange, she would know exactly what was right to do. She would know that she must be strong within, like the pine, yielding and obedient, like the flex-ible bamboo, and, like the plum that blossoms under the snow, gently persevering.

As it was—how could she know the right way to act in a Christian school, taught by foreigners? She had never even seen a foreigner! How was she to avoid dis-gracing her family by other-than-expected behavior?

"Niisan," she asked timidly, "will it be all right in the

new school to try to be like the pine, the bamboo, and the plum?"

He answered thoughtfully, "The pine, bamboo, and plum qualities would be welcome anywhere, Shizuko. But there are other qualities, as well—you are ten now, Shizuko?"

"Yes, I am ten."

"You're too young to understand—and yet, I wonder if you wouldn't?" Yataro half-murmured to himself. "When I went to Tokyo to study, Shizuko, I was very proud. Like you, I have a quick mind, and I had studied the Chinese classics and our own history and literature. I thought the knowledge of the ages was my lasting treasure. Then I learned of Western things and I coveted this modern knowledge, as well. So I took a class in English from the newly-arrived foreigner, Joseph Cosand."

Shizu nodded. All this she knew. It was to Joseph Cosand's school that she was going.

"Mr. Cosand taught the Christian religion, along with English, and at first it was very objectionable to me. I believed it to be both unfilial and even a little stupid. Moreover, I had read enough about Western countries to know that the kindness and mercy extolled in Christian doctrine didn't seem to make much difference in the national history of these countries. But I was very curious about the new ideas. Do you understand how I could be?"

"No, I don't," Shizu answered vigorously.

Yataro laughed, but not unkindly. "Well, I suppose

not. But this you will understand. I was rude to Mr. Cosand. I constantly made fun of his religion, mocked him, tripped up his tongue in Japanese, even—I can scarcely bring myself to think of it now—laid pitfalls for him in the school so he would stumble and look ridiculous before the students!"

Shizu drew her breath sharply, but she was not altogether surprised. To mock a teacher was to break one of Confucius's strongest rules. But the "rough spirit" sometimes took control of Yataro.

"Can you imagine what Mr. Cosand did to me for this?"

Shizu could only wait in dread for Yataro to continue. Her teacher at the Cherry River Grammar School once had been so displeased with her for moving her feet during a lesson that he had rapped her hands with a ruler in sight of the whole class.

"Nothing!" Yataro almost whispered. "Do you understand? Nothing! He would only look at me with a patient smile and then go on about his business. Finally, I went and asked him to tell me more about this Christianity."

"Oh!" Shizu softly exclaimed. Her mother had told her many times that she must ignore any efforts of the school to teach her the Christian religion. It had been only a dozen years since the death-ban for Christians had been lifted. It was a dangerous religion.

The bearers had stopped to rest at the top of a long hill. Below them the rice fields stretched down like giant steps, and beyond was a village, its thatch-roofed brown houses half hidden by the trees, the tiered roof of its temple a scarlet slash against the pines. Far away the blue of Tokyo Bay glimmered in the sun.

"And I became a Christian," Yataro said quietly.

Shizu could hardly breathe. "Does Father know?"

"Yes, Father knows. Not Mother. She wouldn't be able to understand."

And neither do I, Shizu thought, memories of home crowding her mind. So many recollections were linked to family worship. Like the days of Obon, when the warm presence of the ancestors were welcomed back into the family with feasts and prayers, and then guided back again on their souls' journey by tiny candles that they all lighted together—Yataro, too. How could he become a Christian? She looked straight ahead, saying nothing.

The steepness of the hills forced them to travel in separate rickshas when they started up again, but every time the bearers stopped for rest, Yataro jumped down and came over to join his sister. He didn't say much, but his concern and kindness gradually made her forget her resentment at his new-found religion.

Toward evening, they reached the small inn where they were to spend the night. Shizu could hardly wait for her bath. After the long day's travel, the unhappiness and fears, Shizu found more than the usual comfort in the familiar ritual. First the thorough scrubbing by the jolly maid, and then the long, relaxing soak in hot water to her chin. Later, dressed in a loose, cool, after-bath kimono, Shizu joined Yataro in their room. They ate their dinner there, savoring the specialty of the little mountain inn, the fresh trout caught in the fast running stream nearby.

Yataro moved his table and cushion next to Shizu, and they sat together on the matted floor, watching the cascading water through the half-opened *shōji*.

After the maid had taken away the food and the low tables, and had brought out the sleeping quilts, Shizu prodded her brother to talk. She felt drowsy but she wasn't quite ready for sleep.

"Talk to me, Niisan. Tell me of your friends in Tokyo. Have you seen Father's cousin Reisaburo Kondo lately?"

"Oh, no, he's much too busy to come to Tokyo and talk with students. He spends all his time at the Yokosuka Naval Base. He is working on plans for the battleship *Akagi*. I believe it will be the first gunboat we've ever built in Japan from our own plans."

"He can speak English, can't he?"

"Oh, yes, and several other languages. He went to Scotland, you know, and studied ship-building in Glasgow."

"Now tell me about our grandfather Higuchi."

"Oh, you know that story. You tell it to me!"

"No, I want to hear it," Shizu insisted.

So he told it. "When our grandfather was an aide to Lord Hoshino, there was great unrest. The Black Ships of Admiral Perry had come, and the Americans, English, and Russians were all demanding that Japan open its ports to commerce. At first everyone said, 'No, keep out!' But the Black Ships came back, and their power was unmistakable. As always happens when people are afraid and don't know what to do, the lords began to quarrel and fight among themselves. One group wanted to keep Japan closed against the foreigners; another believed that Japan should abandon her old ways and strive to become a modern nation. Lord Hoshino's group felt so strongly that they raised an army to support their views. Grandfather commanded Lord Hoshino's forces when they went into battle. They lost, and Grandfather, to save his lord from disgrace, took all the blame himself. He wrote a letter to the victorious commander, saying: 'The defeat was my fault. Please forgive my lord.' And then he ceremonially killed himself."

"Oh, wasn't it a brave thing to do!" exclaimed Shizu.

"Yes," said Yataro slowly. "It was. It was the highest good our grandfather knew—to sacrifice his life."

"And now he is honored in his village," Shizu added proudly, "with incense always burning before his tomb."

"Yes, he was the last to commit *seppuku* before the new laws were passed, forbidding it. In the old days, a samurai was supposed to take his own life when he was disgraced. There are so many famous stories about it that I doubt that you could have heard them all. Shall I tell you another one, to put you sound asleep, Shizuko?"

As Yataro spoke, Shizu stretched out in the sleeping position decreed for families of the samurai. Flat on her back, a little wooden pillow placed carefully under her neck, her arms straight at her sides, she listened to her brother until his story blurred in dreams.

When Yataro saw she was asleep, he closed his lips on the old story and sat thinking as darkness came into the room.

He had given little Shizu quite a shock today, but he had thought she needed some preparation. Now, when she met the Cosands, she would remember what forbearance Joseph Cosand had shown her brother. Perhaps Christianity would not be quite so frightening.

Shizu was a sturdy little character. With her fine mind, if she became a Christian too, who knew what she might accomplish!

Soon then his thoughts turned to his own purposes and visions. He would go on with his course in architecture at the Imperial University and when he was established in his profession, he would try to wield influence in the affairs of his country, just as his cousin Reisaburo was beginning to do. He would travel, like Inazo Nitobe, and learn all the best from all the world to build into the new Japan. He would open the hearts of his countrymen to the Christian message of brotherhood.

While Shizu slept, Yataro dreamed. But hers was to be the opportunity to carry his message and in some measure to live his dreams.

CHAPTER TWO

The Uncertain Rebel

Shizu was young, and the school was young. They grew together, and at first the growth was so fast that it was hard for the Cosands to keep up.

Joseph and Sarah Ann Cosand had come to Japan, a part of that dynamic missionary effort that characterized the Japan of the 1880's. Joseph had begun teaching English in a government school, and soon his friend Sen Tsuda offered him a house in which to start the girls' school they had come so far to establish.

In the first class, besides Shizu Higuchi, who was the youngest, there were Moto Takane and Iku Suzuki. Sen Tsuda's wife and daughter, Ume, also enrolled.

Mr. Cosand taught the girls English and Bible, Mrs. Cosand taught them sewing and knitting. But these classes were far from being the only activities sheltered by the little house.

Along with interest in the West, Japan felt some resentment toward it. The first treaties, signed in 1858, concerned commerce, currency exchange, and diplomatic relations. When the statesmen of Japan had time to gain perspective, they discovered that many features of these treaties were unilateral and seemed most unfair. There was, for example, the lack of Japanese sovereignty in the tariff agreements, and no provision had been made for treaty revision. Moreover, the extraterritoriality clause gave foreigners the protection of their own coun' try's laws, rather than making them subject to Japanese law. This meant that sometimes a foreigner could break the law in Japan and not be punished.

When the Japanese protested, foreign governments shrugged off their complaints.

"Your economy is too undeveloped. Your laws are too backward," they said. Or again, "Your punishments are too barbarous, your justice is too uncertain."

For many years, young Japanese listened to these criticisms and counter-criticisms, and turned back to examine their own ways and to plan for reform. In this ferment of study, they found help in discussions with friendly foreign missionaries.

Sometimes so much was going on in Sen Tsuda's house that even the sliding paper panels that could close off additional rooms weren't equal to giving privacy to every group. One day two gentlemen were ushered by Joseph Cosand into a small room where a little girl was already sitting on the floor reading a book.

When the little girl saw them come in, she got up and bowed and started to go away.

"No, Shizuko," said Mr. Cosand, putting his hand gently on her shoulder (a type of demonstrative friend' liness Shizu had learned by now to accept without flinch' ing), "there is really no other place for you to study. My friends won't mind your sitting quietly near, and I hope we won't disturb your studying. Mr. Nitobe, Mr. Uchimura, this is Shizuko Higuchi, a very earnest pupil."

Shizu bowed again, sank down, and looked fixedly at her book. But the words on the page became meaningless, as Shizu could not help following the conversation of the men. Unfortunately they spoke English, and Shizu could understand only part of what they said.

"Well, friends," Mr. Cosand said, "you see, we've done it—what you suggested that day in Philadelphia. We've made a start, though a small one."

"And what has your reception been?" asked Inazo Nitobe.

"Really splendid," Mr. Cosand replied. "The interest is intense, and among all kinds of people. Sometimes they stop me in the street to ask me questions, and the shrewdest sort of questions, too, which shows they have been thinking."

"Do you remember," Kanzo Uchimura asked, "what Francis Xavier wrote from Japan to Ignatius Loyola, in 1549? Something about—let me see—sending only patient men as teachers? What was it exactly? It escapes me."

"Send me patient men," Mr. Nitobe took it up at once. "They will be persecuted—persecuted by questions, at all hours of day and night. They will not have time for prayer, meditation, Mass, hardly time to keep alive. These people question and argue without any idea of time, so they can have answers to communicate to others. And he ended—I don't remember it word for word, but this is the idea— They are the delight of my soul." [1]

Mr. Nitobe, glancing over Mr. Cosand's shoulder, met Shizu's fascinated eyes. Oh, if she could only understand a little more! Their English went so fast.

Mr. Nitobe's face warmed with a smile. "Why, little girl, you would like to know what we are saying!" he said in Japanese. "Let me tell you." And he told her.

"And who was Francis Xavier?" asked Shizu.

The three men laughed heartily. Shizu looked from one to another, and decided they were probably laughing because she was asking questions, just as Francis Xavier had said the Japanese did.

"*Gomen kudasai,* I'm sorry," she said soberly.

"You need never apologize for wishing knowledge, Shizuko," Mr. Cosand said. "This is a longing given by God. I will answer your question. Francis Xavier was a Jesuit, a Roman Catholic missionary, who came here in 1549. He loved the Japanese people, as you have heard, and so did the other Jesuits who came. They made many converts, some say a million, before Hideyoshi, who was in power then, suddenly ordered the missionaries to leave Japan at once. Perhaps he had been listening to gossip against the Christians and feared foreign conquest."

"Did they all leave?" Shizu asked with mounting curiosity.

[1] *Life and Letters of St. Francis Xavier,* by Henry James Coleridge.

"No, but those who stayed had a hard time of it and so did their Japanese followers. By the seventeenth century ill will had become widespread and persecutions were very severe."

"Were all the Christians killed?" Shizu almost whispered her question. It had suddenly become terribly important to know whether everyone, even people like Joseph Cosand, had been put to death.

"Some escaped, and passed on the faith for many years. It is said that the *goningumi* system of organization by five-family groups was begun in the Tokugawa era in an effort to root out Christianity."

The men turned back to resume their conversation. By listening hard, Shizu got some idea of their concerns. It seemed to her that they were anxious about the future, although she was too young to really grasp the import of their fears.

"Now, people are responsive; later a reaction will come," Mr. Nitobe said. "Already there is much resentment about the treaties."

Mr. Cosand nodded. "One can't blame Townsend Harris, who negotiated with the Japanese government," he observed. "He couldn't have done better with his limited knowledge of the Japanese people. He was working in the dark. But the treaty is unfair."

"Moreover," Mr. Nitobe added, "trouble brews to North and West. Korea is unstable, and points like a dagger at Japan. At any time, China or Russia might grasp that dagger. This danger gives the military extremists power in our government, and they're always

ready to use their power at the expense of all foreigners."

"I see these dangers," Mr. Cosand answered. "That's
why we're making what haste we can in building our
work now. But we must have more room. We want to
build a school and meetinghouse—yet as foreigners, we
can't buy our own land."

"That is true, and we can help you, there." Kanzo
Uchimura was enthusiastic. "A Christian Japanese law-
yer here in Tokyo will work out the details. We came to
urge you to proceed with this as soon as possible."

"We'll do it," cried Mr. Cosand. "We'll do it!
There's a piece of land we've had our eye on in Shiba
ward—Hijirizaka, they call it; a good omen—Saints'
Hill!"

"Let's not deal in omens," Mr. Nitobe demurred.
"That property you speak of once belonged to a
Buddhist temple. It was struck by lightning and burned
to ashes; rebuilt, struck by lightning again, and burned
once more. The Buddhists gave it up."

"Where the Buddhists have given up, let the Friends
make their start!" Joseph Cosand exclaimed.

The men left, remembering to bow to Shizu, who
gave them her deepest obeisance. Afterward she sat for
a long time, her book closed, pondering all that had been
said.

Shizu soon learned that the Friends had been successful in acquiring the land they had spoken of that day,
and she, like everyone else, was eager to see the place.
It was arranged that the school should make an expedi-

tion to see it, and by chance it turned out to be on the day of Jugoya, the August moon-viewing festival.

Shizu was delighted, though it wouldn't be the same as at home. Her teachers enjoyed the beauty of nature, but not with Japanese feeling. The missionaries always seemed too bound up with other thoughts. But anyway, it would be fun to have a picnic.

The cook at the school packed up elaborate food boxes, one for each, and they all set out in rickshas for Saint's Hill. It was a beautiful autumn day, and people along the way were singing as they went about their everyday tasks, and the special preparations for the evening's festival. Everyone was happy that the sky was clear to welcome the full moon. The rickshas went on and on until they reached an open field on the top of a ridge. The red roof of a fox shrine peered out of trees on the right. Beyond, to the West, rose up the beloved cone of Fuji-san. This was Saint's Hill. Shizu and the others walked all around, viewing the site from every vantage point.

Later, they sat on cushions on the hill and ate their meal. Voices but faintly heard, songs of crickets and birds, a barking dog—commonplace enough—were transformed by twilight into haunting beauty. A few white sails bobbed far out on Tokyo Bay. And then the moon rose. This was the awaited glory—the full harvest moon. Everyone sat in silence.

Finally Shizu said softly, "I see Usagi-san, the hare who lives in the moon."

"A hare? In America we think it is a man," Sarah

Ann Cosand answered. "Can't you see his eyes and nose and mouth? His face is rather crooked, I admit!"

"Yes, it is," agreed Shizu. "But you also have to use imagination to see the hare, on his hind legs, pounding rice. Anyway, this is a wonderful place from which to greet him. I hope we can move soon!"

They did move soon, by the beginning of the next year, 1887. Their first buildings were a large, foreign-style school and a teachers' residence.

New students came, and new teachers. Miss Mary Ann Gundry from England came. She was full of ideas.

"How would you like to be King's Daughters?" she asked the girls one day.

They surveyed her. What could she mean? Pert little Chiyo, a new student whom Shizu admired for her liveliness and ready tongue, answered, "We have no king in this country."

That was as close as one could politely come to saying that they were all daughters of the Emperor, who was a remote, god-like father to all his people. Lesser countries could have kings.

Miss Gundry drew rather a deep breath. "I mean, of course, that we are all children of God. We think of him symbolically as king of our lives. In this club we would be a group of girls who were trying to serve God like loyal daughters. Serving God means helping people, and in order to earn money to help those in need, we can knit and do other handwork."

The girls nodded. They loved handwork. Some of them thought no more about the idea of the King's

Daughters, or else placidly accepted it, but Shizu pondered it.

The King's Daughters had a good time. When there was a spare hour between classes or after studying was finished, the girls could hurry to Miss Gundry's room. Miss Gundry's room was friendly. Shizu couldn't think it pretty, it was so cluttered up with this and that. But there were many comfortable cushions to sit on, lamps that gave good light, plates of cookies and candy to nibble—and always fun. Sometimes the girls would knit while someone read aloud in English. Often one of them would turn to Shizu and whisper, "What's that word in Japanese?" Shizu always understood so well.

Most of the stories were about Jesus. Shizu listened with intense, if rebellious interest. Since Yataro had turned against their parents by becoming a Christian then it was up to Shizu to be doubly staunch. Yet what she heard was appealing. It was hard not to feel well acquainted with Jesus.

When time came for the holidays, she and Yataro traveled home together.

"You have enjoyed the year at school, Shizuko?" Yataro asked.

"Yes, I have enjoyed it."

"You have learned a great deal?"

"Yes, I have learned a great deal."

"But you are glad to be going home?"

"Oh, yes! I am glad to be going home!" Shizu's face broke into smiles at the thought of slipping back into accustomed habits, understanding every word that was spoken, and not having to remember to do things differently.

Their parents beamed with joy to see them again. Tami, as soon as the girls were alone, bubbled with questions, but soon lost interest in the answers. Mother cooked Yataro's and Shizu's favorite foods, and after the meal listened closely as Shizu answered her father's questions.

"Do you have classes in gymnastics, such as I have heard of?"

"Yes," said Shizu, getting up and pushing her arms out vigorously from her chest in all directions to illustrate. Then she caught her mother's horrified glance and sank quickly into a more appropriate pose.

Her father chuckled. "They are beginning to teach calisthenics in the public schools, also," he said. "It is good for the health."

"I'm growing," Shizu said. "I keep well even if the schoolrooms are warmly heated."

"They are!" repeated Tami, looking down instinctively at her feet, which always grew so cold during the winter, when the hardest, longest lessons were done.

"And I can study very well, even though I am comfortable," Shizu confided. "It's hard to believe."

"Are their manners very dreadful?" asked Mother in a low voice.

"At first I thought so," Shizu answered. "The teachers almost run. They hurry up the steps, talk with their hands, and smile and laugh a great deal. The women are served first at table, and walk first through doors, and when Mrs. Cosand wants her shawl, she says, 'Joseph, will you fetch my shawl, please?' "

"You see," complained the mother to her husband, "her marriage prospects will be ruined."

"Oh, Shizuko will behave in a proper fashion and there will be no problems," answered Mr. Higuchi. "You remember the precepts of Confucius, my child?"

"I remember the five duties, between master and servant, father and son, husband and wife, brother and brother, and between two friends. I presume that means daughter and sister, too?" Shizu added. She caught a twinkle in her father's eye; at least he wasn't displeased at her boldness.

"See, she remembers. Are you learning well, Shizuko? That's the main thing. Let's hear your English."

Shizu answered promptly:

> *Oh the bitter pain and sorrow*
> *That a time could ever be*
> *When I proudly said to Jesus*
> *All of self and none of thee.*

Then she caught her breath and looked quickly at her father.

She had repeated the words from this often-sung hymn because she knew she could say them faster than anything else, but suddenly she realized their meaning.

However, her father, who could read only a little English and speak even fewer words with effort, was entirely thrown off by Shizu's fluency. "She is learning well. There is nothing to fear."

Shizu let out her held breath as quietly as she could, realizing for the first time that she would feel terribly disappointed if she couldn't go back to the Girls' School.

Next day a family meeting was called. No reason was given, but Shizu knew it had to do with Yataro's becoming a Christian. The relatives came; uncles and male cousins gathered behind the closed *shōji,* and the angry murmur of their voices drifted out to Shizu, playing with Tami in the garden.

Would Yataro be disinherited? The thought made Shizu shudder. To be put out of the family in a land where a person is only a fragment, is worse than death. Even now, when many things had changed; even for Yataro, whose thoughts were strong and independent. Now Shizu understood why he had not talked more on the trip home.

Just then someone slid back the *shōji,* and Shizu saw that tea was being served. Standing with her head turned aside, so as not to stare, she could feel the atmosphere of the room. Quiet, and sober; the anger seemed dissipated.

Afterward, Yataro told Shizu that their father's mildness had saved the day. Agreeing at one point with the uncles, at the next with Yataro, he had made their differences seem smaller.

"I think if he were younger, Father himself would become a Christian," Yataro added.

During the holidays they celebrated Obon, the annual festival in honor of the spirits of the departed. Shizu joined in the preparations, helping to clean the family graves and decorate the altar-shelf, and finally in the ceremony of farewell, when little fires were lighted in all the gateways of the town.

But when the family had gone to the temple, Yataro's invisible withdrawal seemed to Shizu to frighten off the ancestral ghosts, whose presence she had always felt before.

"Niisan, please come and speak to me," she begged the day after the little rush boats had been launched at dawn to carry away the beloved spirits.

Yataro smiled at her troubled face, as he nodded assent to her request.

Shizu dipped her head in sudden embarrassment.

"Niisan, I am miserable," she burst out. "How can I know what's right? Last year during Obon I did not doubt that the spirits of our departed were all about me, but this year I only wondered if they were really there, and it seemed quite doubtful that they were!"

"Does it matter so much whether they were really there or not?" Yataro asked. "Wasn't it remembering them lovingly that counted?"

"But if they weren't there, what has happened to them? What will happen to us? When we bow at the altar-shelf, isn't there even one *hotokesama,* one family spirit?"

"Isn't it better to have one God over all instead of just family spirits?" Yataro asked. "Such a God as Jesus tells of, loving each one of us, and always near? He even counts the sparrows and knows when each one falls. Surely he will care for us."

Shizu began to cry. "But Mother would be so unhappy to have me change my ideas, stop revering the ancestors," she sobbed.

"Shizuko," said her brother, "do you really think it's wrong to wonder if there is one God? You've heard the teachers speak of George Fox, haven't you? Once he said that every time your heart is hungry, or that you're dissatisfied with yourself, or that you think you've done wrong, or fallen short—it shows the Divine Spirit is visiting your soul!"

"But—but must you always be wondering, then?"

"No," said Yataro. "God has put his truth in every one of us. We may not find it easily, or always, but it is there, and he has given us the means to find it."

A feeling, not quite of understanding, but of reassurance, came to Shizu. As it often happened, a poem came to her mind that seemed to express what she felt:

> *From plum-scented veil*
> *Of haze, suddenly rose the sun*
> *On the mountain trail.*[1]

Yataro nodded as Shizu recited the familiar words. "That's right. The light comes and shows what you must do. I hope the mountain trails aren't too steep—and yet they will be steep, Shizuko."

When the vacation was over and Shizu bowed her farewells to the family, she felt guilty as well as sad at leaving them, for she was beginning to understand her mother's unspoken grief. But she was happy when she

[1] "On the Mountain Trail" by Bashō, 1644–1694. In *A Pepper-Pod* by Kenneth Yasuda. N. Y., Alfred A. Knopf, 1947. Used by permission.

got back to the school, and she ran from room to room to greet everyone.

That night when she went to bed, the roll that held her *obi* in place fell to the floor and burst open. Hundreds of folded paper prayers rolled out.

There was silence as her roommates paused in their undressing to gaze on these little signs of a mother's love and fear.

Shizu's first feeling was embarrassment, but it soon passed. She looked at the little paper things, and slow tears filled her eyes.

Poor Mother, to have to depend on these, and not to know that God was always as near as breathing, to the seeking mind.

CHAPTER THREE

The Gratitude Years

Shizu was graduated at seventeen, and began her "gratitude years." She had been partly supported by the school throughout her course, and now owed two years of service in return. She undertook her assignment with eagerness for she had become a convinced Quaker and was devoted to the school. One of her tasks was to interpret for the new teacher, Miss Minnie Pickett, who arrived in October, 1893.

Miss Pickett was small and lively. As soon as Shizu saw her she thought of a singing cricket. Shizu and some of the older students went to call as soon as the new teacher had had time to rest.

Miss Pickett opened the door to their knock, made a profound bow, and brought her head up smack against Shizu's.

"Oh, excuse me!" she cried. "But how in the world do you say that in Japanese?"

"Oh," said Shizu, smiling, "we speak English."

"Do you? That's wonderful!" Miss Pickett made them come in and sit down. "I've felt so strange ever since I left the boat. There's no pier, you know, so they just drop you over the side into a sampan. I was prepared for a plunge into the water! But I landed all right. The sampan sailor was kind and friendly, but we could only talk by signs."

Miss Pickett made all sorts of signs till the girls were giggling with her. "I don't believe even signs are the same in Japanese! Am I talking too fast? I never knew before this trip how quick a foreign tongue can sound!"

"Perhaps you are a little quick," Shizu acknowledged.

More slowly, Miss Pickett described her journey from San Francisco on the *S. S. Peru*. There had been storms, but Miss Pickett, staying well, had found them exciting. She described meeting the captain, strolling on the deck during the few hours of calm, and listening to concerts in the lounge.

Then she asked the girls their names and repeated them, with slow and labored emphasis, looking intently at each girl as she spoke. She was determined to learn Japanese and this was a beginning. I don't understand, *wakarimasen,* became a constant expression.

Actually she learned very fast. She was never afraid to try a a new word or phrase. She told them they could laugh at her, for she knew she was funny, and that then they must correct her. Shizu was astounded at first—to be proper was so important, and ridicule had seemed a condemnation. But Miss Pickett said a good teacher must be a good learner. This idea, so strange at first, on second thought seemed good and sound.

And it was always so much fun to be with Miss Pickett. She was interested in everything Shizu had to tell her and as the months went by, they became good friends.

"The *namazu* is surely wriggling this morning!" Shizu remarked to her one day. Slight earthquake tremors were frequent in Tokyo, but on that day there'd been several. "That's the great catfish that holds the islands on its back, you know."

"I didn't know, but I surely can believe it!" Miss Pickett answered vehemently. "I've become used to the little quakes in the year I've been here, but gracious, this is really strong! Do you think we should go to the parlor?"

The jolting was increasing in frequency and vigor. Tiles began to slide off the roof, falling with sharp, repeated crashes. Girls came running from all over to the big parlor, where Shizu and Miss Pickett had already come.

"There are two kinds of earthquake motion, the horizontal, and the more dangerous, the vertical," said Shizu soberly. Everyone could tell that the present movement was sharply vertical.

"Pickett *sensei,* teacher, may we escape?" asked one of the girls politely in a trembling voice.

"My dear girls, to run would be sheer folly," said a strong voice from the hall. Miss Haines, one of the older missionaries, stood in the entrance. "Don't you hear the tiles falling? You'd be struck the minute you stepped out."

Defiantly a picture swung from the wall and smashed.

The girl who was so frightened ran past Miss Haines and tried to open the front door.

"They're all locked, my dears," said Miss Haines calmly. "Let's sing, shall we?"

They sang into the uproar; when a lull came, their song burst forth until the tumult drowned it again. They sang as if their lives depended on it, whether it could be heard or not. In that time of terror, Shizu had the steadying thought that this was the way Christians lived, with harmony and purpose, whether the world crashed and banged around them or was still.

Gradually the shock and sound diminished. The explosive bursts became less frequent and less severe. There was something dead and ominous in the stillness that succeeded the earthquake.

The girls went outside to join Mr. Cosand and some of the other men as they surveyed the damage, but they were soon alarmed by a new sound—the terrifying sound of fire-bells.

Japan, a land of wood and paper, always organized against this potent foe, each village having arrangements made ahead of time for everyone to bear a bucket, and each city having watchtowers and neighborhood fire companies. But everyone knew that the power belonged to the fire—the fire and the wind.

Before this new onslaught, the girls were silent. They helped to get their own equipment ready and stood dumbly watching the raging horror of the flames. The blue waters of the bay were hidden by clouds of smoke, and soon billows of it rolled up the hill, shooting out wicked streamers of red that entwined the little thatch-roofed houses and turned them into blazing torches.

And then the wind turned. The fire raced off in another direction, leaving only stray flames to run languidly along the fence that edged the mission compound until they finally sputtered out under water from the school's bucket brigade.

The meetinghouse and school were safe.

A few hours later the fire on the hillside had burned itself out. Survivors returned to pick their way through the ashes and acrid smoke, searching hopelessly for any salvage. There was practically nothing left, except on the top of Saint's Hill. There stood the foreign buildings, brazenly untouched.

Students and teachers were gathered in the meetinghouse, having a service of thanksgiving, when their peaceful devotion was broken by a rising hum. Hurrying to the windows, the worshipers saw a mob rushing up the hill toward them. Hysterical over their own losses and infuriated that the holocaust had spared the compound, the dispossessed streamed up the hill, screaming imprecations as they ran.

"It was a mistake!" shouted one, his blue gown blackened and torn. "It was a mistake! The gods would have us rectify it!"

Almost more shocked than frightened by this audacity, Shizu watched him thrust a stick into some embers and lift it up, a blazing torch. Several others quickly followed his example.

"Burn out the foreign demons! Drive them away!"

Miss Pickett was standing next to Shizu, shivering violently. Suddenly she took a deep breath, and was quiet.

"They're going out," she said.

Shizu saw Chuzo Kaifu, the principal, a frail figure in his dark kimono, and Mr. Cosand, leave the doorway and stand before the onrushing men. The mob closed in on them, but as Mr. Kaifu held up his hand, its pace gradually slackened.

"My friends," he said, "we know you're homeless and afraid. Since God has spared our meetinghouse, we know he wants us to use it for him. There is no better way than to invite you in. You may live here until your homes can be rebuilt."

Like a wave drawn backward from the shore, a long astonished exclamation washed over the crowd as they heard the invitation. The fierce, smoke-blackened leader stood silent a moment, then spoke.

"*Sensei,* teacher," he said. "We do not understand, yet we accept. Some of us can find refuge with relatives, but those who cannot will come here to stay and will be thankful."

With remarkably little confusion, the crowd sorted itself into families, divided up the space in the meeting-house, and apportioned the quilts and blankets that were brought to them by the servants and students of the school.

The testimony of faith and service during the earth-quake and fire drew several of the curious to the meet-inghouse, and in the passing weeks and months, some of these became deeply interested in the faith whose fruit they had already tasted.

Shizu herself had become a regular attendant at Meeting, and often saw Yataro there. Even in that quiet and orderly place, however, one could feel ripples from a storm that was rising in the country.

One day, at the session of the Monthly Meeting, these ripples suddenly broke into heavy surf.

A young Japanese, who had recently become an enthusiastic member, rose to make a resolution.

"In view of the fact that the war now pending against the Chinese—as punishment for their unjust disrespect for Japan in regard to Korea—is a just war, I propose that members of this Meeting be free to support the government in its prosecution of the war."

There followed an empty silence.

Shizu felt tossed about by the beating of her heart. Half of her mind understood and echoed what the young man said. Within her, as in all her countrymen, was rooted the idea of *kokutai*—the bond uniting all Japanese in blood-relationship and loyalty. How could she turn against her country?

Yet she, like all the other members of the Meeting, had signed the Believers' Book, which meant assenting to the Friends' Peace Principles.

Joseph Cosand stood up. He said quietly, "I think perhaps the whole meaning of this resolution has not yet come to our friend. Would it not be well to hold over the resolution till next month? That will give us time to think it over carefully."

Yataro and Shizu went out of the Meeting together, and by common consent returned to the school residence to discuss the matter.

For a while they sat in troubled silence. Then Shizu asked, "Niisan, what is going to happen? Surely Christianity is doomed in Japan if all the Christians refuse to carry out the ancient principles of our country. There will be persecution again, and all our gains will be destroyed."

Yataro answered gravely, "Very likely that is true. I see in a hundred ways that the old Japanese ideas again predominate. I don't fear persecution—I fear tradition and habit. For this very reason we must stand out against this insidious attack on the pure meaning of Christianity."

Shizu exclaimed, "Niisan, do you mean—that you would not fight in the war?"

Yataro answered, "Shizuko, I signed the Believers' Book and agreed with the Peace Principles. I did it from my heart. The love Christ showed us, love without constraint or boundaries, love for all men everywhere, is the most important thing in life to me. If they make me go into the army, I shall shoot into the air."

At the next Monthly Meeting the resolution came up for discussion. Joseph Cosand and the other missionaries were not there to argue the point. They had decided that, as visitors in the country, they could not participate in such a decision. It was a question for the conscience of the Japanese people themselves.

This time the resolution passed. Many members resigned. The remnant was too small to carry on. A new group had to form, and start the work again.

Shizu felt both frightened and invigorated. She had escaped from a cocoon of old ideas, smooth, comforting —and confining. But her new wings felt frail and weak. She could only hope that in time they would gain strength like Yataro's.

Before very long, before he could even use those powerful wings, while he was still a student in the university, Yataro died.

> *Together with one blossom more,*
> *Oh! Life, thou goest on thy way.*[1]

[1] Onitsura, 1661–1738. In *Japanese Poetry,* by Basil Chamberlain.

CHAPTER FOUR

The Turtle-neck Sweater

"Shizuko! Mr. Miyamori's here for his lesson."

"Thank you, Tamiko. I never know whether to be delighted or scared about that." Shizu gave her little sister a friendly look as she went out. She was glad Tami had come to the school, several years ago, for together they had been able to bear more easily the many griefs that had come to them.

Yataro's death had been in some ways the most stunning blow to Shizu. He had been counselor and guide to her, as well as brother. But then, to have both mother and father go within a year! It had been very hard. And though there were uncles and cousins left, the tie was not as close as it would have been if the two girls had not forsaken traditional Japanese ways to become Christians. They felt very much alone, except for their warm Quaker friends.

It was difficult, as Shizu had said, to tell whether she was more excited or frightened by the lessons with Asataro Miyamori. Joseph Cosand was supposed to be the teacher, and Shizu to assist by interpreting. But the

Japanese part of the lesson was so very complicated, as
Mr. Miyamori explained his brilliant and unusual ideas,
that Mr. Cosand was often left far behind. Shizu felt
that she was far behind, too, even when she understood
the words.

Mr. Miyamori was awaiting her impatiently with a
leather volume in his hands. He held it up. "I have found
this! A Japanese translation of part of Shakespeare's
plays. As you know, I have been working on an English
version myself, and I must say that this translation
doesn't satisfy me at all. Come here and let me tell you
what I mean."

They were deep in discussion of the book when Mr.
Cosand came in. "What seems to be the trouble?" he
asked them with a smile.

"This translation! There is no real understanding,"
Mr. Miyamori cried. "It is the classic mind that is the
trouble—this man is translating Shakespeare into Chinese forms of thought before he brings it over into Japanese. In between, somewhere—poof! Shakespeare gets
lost."

Joseph Cosand looked bewildered by this flood of
Japanese, and Shizu tried to make it clear to him.

"Mr. Miyamori thinks it would be better to bring
over the meaning into Japanese ways of thought. He
thinks Shakespeare wrote as English people of his day
spoke. He thinks Shakespeare's ideas should be put into
Japanese as it is commonly spoken, even if sometimes
you have to use different words."

"An idea. A real idea. I've heard some Westerners

discuss it, too," said Mr. Cosand. "Now let's see what you would do here. Take this passage from Hamlet—"

They were off. The time sped by, and none of them paid any attention. Someone called softly, without response, and had to call again.

It was Tami. "The Binfords have come!"

"Oh! I must welcome them!" Shizu cried eagerly, bundling up her books.

"You are eager to see these new arrivals from America!" Mr. Miyamori remarked. "Sometimes it seems to me that you are always facing toward the West. What are you going to do with your life, Higuchi-san? Will you be willing to marry and fit humbly into a Japanese woman's subordinate position?"

Shizu paused and frowned thoughtfully. "I try not to wonder. I should like to study more. To study, and learn, and teach—I simply must teach. Yet a woman should marry, too." Her brow smoothed. "But you see, I mustn't wonder: God will open it to me. Now I must hurry! I'll be with you again next week."

She bowed a somewhat sketchy bow, and disappeared.

"Even the bow is Western," Mr. Miyamori murmured thoughtfully to Mr. Cosand.

"Sometimes we wonder if we have done wrong in letting Shizu grow so like us," Joseph Cosand answered.

Shizu went on to find the Binfords. Gurney Binford she knew well from his former four-year term of duty at the Friends' Mission. She had interpreted for him. She knew of his many activities—his teaching in the School for Christian Workers (a young men's school), in her own Girls' School, in a Government Fisheries School, and his supervision of a little primary school in the slums that he ran and supported himself.

She had watched him work at top speed from four-thirty in the morning till eleven-thirty at night and still feel that he wasn't doing enough. She had not been surprised when his health broke, and he had to go back to America.

And now he had returned with a wife! Shizu looked shyly into the room where the Binfords were holding an informal reception.

Gurney Binford caught sight of her. "Come in, Shizuko Higuchi! Come and meet my wife!" he cried.

Shizu came in and met Mrs. Binford, and was much pleased with her gentle, friendly way. How happy the two were together, and with what deep understanding they smiled at each other! Throughout the pleasant welcome services and festivities, Shizu shared the warm feeling of the group.

"And now, Mr. and Mrs. Binford, I hope you will live in Japan as long as you can," said Asataro Miyamori, who was making the welcoming speech.

Again that warm and comprehending look flashed between the new husband and wife. Somehow, Shizu felt very lonely.

Mr. Miyamori had made great progress when the next lesson came around. He had been trying his own translation of Hamlet, and though his English was not quite equal to the task as yet, Shizu knew that he had the ability and persistence to accomplish it in the end.

When the lesson was over, Mr. Miyamori, suddenly quite formal, bowed to Shizu.

"To which of your relatives should I address myself, in case I have communications to put forward regarding your interests?"

He spoke exactly like a go-between.

Shizu mentioned her uncle but asked no questions. As quickly as she could, she hurried off to find Tami to tell her of the turn Mr. Miyamori's lesson had taken.

She and Tami paid a visit shortly to their relatives, in response to a special invitation. After dinner all the younger members of the family, including Tami, were politely brushed out of the room.

The uncle began conversation immediately.

"The gentleman named Asataro Miyamori, for whose English lessons you interpret, came to visit me the other day."

"Oh, did he?" Shizu inquired politely. "A very learned man. A very good English student. He will bring honor to Japan."

If Miyamori-san was acting as a go-between, which now seemed certain, for whom was he acting? That was the burning question.

"I didn't know exactly how to respond to his proposal. You are of samurai blood, high-ranking samurai. To marry into the farmer class would have been imprudent in the former state of affairs. Today, everything is different. The farmers are a sturdy group. Without rice, the country perishes."

A farmer? Well, who was he? Where did he live?

Was he a Christian? Questions raced through her mind, but Shizu sat perfectly still.

"Miyamori-san came up to Tokyo from Hiroshima some years ago with three young friends." Shizu's uncle was enjoying the slow unfolding of the tale, keen-eyed for any signs of unmannerly impatience from his niece. "Two of the young men were brothers, younger sons, with little to look forward to on their father's farm."

Shizu hoped her uncle couldn't see her hands, trembling in her lap.

"One of these brothers studied law, as did the fourth of the companions, and soon they both established themselves. Miyamori, as you know, became a scholar. But the second brother, the youngest of the four. . . ." the uncle shook his head. "He had some idea of becoming an actor. For several years he acted in Kabuki—or maybe it was some other kind of theater—in Kobe, and in Tokyo."

The theater! Of all things far from Shizu's life, or thoughts, or hopes! The theater! Show-case of vanity and empty excitement! And Kabuki, the most popular, gaudy, and bloody of them all! The Kabuki theater in Tokyo was a national institution, its plays half history, half myth. Certain famous roles were passed on from father to son for generations with pride and pomp. But acting was deplored by the Friends missionaries and Shizu shared their feelings.

"Well," said the uncle, after a pause. "He gave up the theater. He was doing well, I understand, had talent —but was just an inch too short. He didn't care for law, so he was apprenticed to a tailoring firm. That big establishment that makes military uniforms, and Western style diplomatic clothes."

An artisan. Shizu breathed again. Well, that was traditionally a lower order than farming, though not so low as the merchant class. It was certainly better than the theater. In these days, things like that didn't matter much. The Samurai had put too much emphasis on class. Besides, she reminded herself, all men were equal in the sight of God.

"He must be an ambitious youth," went on her uncle. "He desired to master other techniques in tailoring, and to make his fortune, I suppose, and to see the world. He went to America."

In spite of her desire to appear calm, and no doubt because of her barbarous lack of training in decorum, Shizu gasped. America!

"He spent a few years there and established himself in a business of his own. He has come home to find a wife, and," the uncle looked at Shizu whimsically, "I know this must surprise you—Miyamori-san wonders whether the family would be interested in your behalf."

Shizu moistened her lips. "Will he return to America?"

"Temporarily. His shop is in Oakland, near San Francisco."

"Isn't that near Berkeley, too, where the University of California is located?" If she were to go to America, she could study! In the United States, women were allowed in the state universities.

"Is this man a Christian?" Shizu's questions raced with her thoughts.

The uncle shrugged. "Well, as to that, I don't know. Having lived in America, no doubt he is."

Shizu could tell that her uncle was favorable to the match. Probably he had been uneasy about her future, hers and Tami's.

As Christians, it was difficult. She was already twenty-four and that was getting old for a Japanese bride. Too, arrangements had to be made for her before Tami's future could be planned. Her voice was low but steady when she put her next question.

"Did Miyamori-san propose a meeting?"

"The young man would be glad to call on you next Sunday night at the teacher's residence."

"On First Day." Shizu bowed assent. "What is his name?"

"His name is Chiyokichi Takahashi."

The orderly practices of First Day passed for Shizu as if it were the first time—or the last. She savored the quiet meals, the meetings, and the songs. How would it be to leave it forever? This had been her life for nearly fourteen years.

She was waiting in her room when Miss Gundry came to call her.

"The young man is here."

"Well?"

"You must judge for yourself."

The two went downstairs together, Shizu trying to retain her customary composure. After all, she didn't have to marry this young man. In fact, this was only a polite, get-acquainted call. They could take a look at each other, and if they weren't satisfied, well . . . They were coming down the stairs. In just a minute now they'd turn at the landing and see him.

There was Mr. Miyamori in his neat, dark, American-style business suit. And there beside him—oh, my!

Such a figure had never before entered the austere hall of the teacher's residence. He was not as tall as Mr. Miyamori, but he made Mr. Miyamori look dull and ordinary. Even the way he stood was gay and audacious. But what was he wearing? His costume wasn't Japanese, and to the best of her knowledge, it wasn't American. Like all the rest of him, it seemed to Shizu that it had style—but so unconventional, so nonchalant! (Afterwards she learned it was a turtle-necked sweater.)

Shizu went blindly through the introductions, and then she found herself sitting beside Miss Gundry, who had taken the conversational initiative. Miss Gundry talked with Mr. Miyamori on neutral topics for a time, and then she fixed Chiyokichi Takahashi with a keen gaze and commenced to question him in her somewhat broken Japanese.

"You have lived in the United State, I have heard. How long?"

Mr. Takahashi lifted his shoulders and tipped his head. Smile wrinkles deepened at the corners of his eyes. "In years, not long. In reference to experience, an age. Such is it to become acquainted with a new country."

Shizu came out of her daze to inquire tentatively

about former friends. "Did you ever meet Dr. Gregory over there? Or the Naylors? The Naylors live in Berkeley; he is president of the First National Bank, and she is a Friends pastor."

"No," said Mr. Takahashi, looking amused. "I met very few Americans, and scarcely any of those I did meet were bank presidents or pastors."

"But—" Shizu said, and then broke off. Certainly his remarks left one with much to puzzle over.

"You found it hard to establish yourself there," Miss Gundry was questioning again, "since you didn't speak English?"

Again the shrug. "To establish myself, yes. To find work, no. Work lay in wait for me at my inn, in the person of the manager, who was also a labor procurer for the railroad. They packed me and some others in a box-car and shipped us—we knew not where. Unloaded, in the midst of a desert, we worked from dawn to dark under a burning sun. We learned the words for 'water,' 'all right,' and 'go home.' This was all we needed to know, for the job. I decided it was not the way to perfect my tailoring, so I went away with two friends—we walked all the way back to Oakland. Oh, I was glad to see those hills again! I decided I must learn some English, so I got a job as a house-boy, in Alameda, and went to school. That was all right, only the people I worked for forgot to feed me now and then. By strange coincidence, those were the same days that their hens forgot to lay!" Even in the formal Japanese language Takahashi was using, his words seemed free and casual.

Mr. Miyamori laughed a little uneasily. Shizu glanced sidewise at Miss Gundry, who smiled, but became serious again right away.

"But you did finally get back into tailoring, didn't you?"

"Oh, yes, I have a shop now," said Mr. Takahashi in an offhand manner. He returned to his story. "My friends got jobs out in Alameda too. We used to walk to Oakland when we had a day off—did a little gambling for amusement."

Mr. Miyamori changed the subject.

"You feel there is a great opportunity in tailoring in California, don't you, Takahashi-san?"

"I'm the only Japanese tailor there, and many Japanese are coming to California every year. I should have plenty of business. Perhaps later I'll go to New York as a cutter. I'll learn what I can, and earn what I can, and then I'll come home, if I wish."

Several of the teachers walked downstairs together, gravely met Mr. Takahashi, and then went out.

"It's time for evening Meeting," explained Shizu, rising. "Will you come with us, Mr. Takahashi?"

"Yes, I'll go anywhere you say," he answered, with a certain emphasis.

Meeting was quieter than usual, with long, meditative pauses between remarks. Perhaps the group felt a little constrained by the presence of Mr. Takahashi, a stranger in a turtle-necked sweater, with intentions on their beloved Shizu. At one time an odd noise—halfway between a cough and a sneeze—broke the silence.

Shizu glanced sideways and saw Mr. Takahashi restoring his countenance to gravity. His eyes twinkled when he saw she'd caught him.

During the rest of the Meeting, Shizu struggled to untangle her thoughts. Was Mr. Takahashi a Christian? Should she ask him even if in his eyes she appeared forward and un-Japanese? Or perhaps it would be better not to know . . .

After the Meeting, Shizu, her indecision resolved, placed herself squarely in front of Mr. Takahashi. Her voice trembled but her manner was firm and compelling. "Are you a Christian?"

Chiyokichi answered without hesitation. "I am not a Christian. I have not come to know that faith. Mine is the religion of our ancestors. I'm grateful for the life that was given me, and I try to find the good in everything."

There was more small talk, but Shizu was wrapped in thought and noticed only a blur of leave-taking.

Miss Gundry came into her room with her, where Tami was already anxiously waiting.

"Well," Miss Gundry remarked flatly, "he won't do, of course."

Shizu watched her, as she stood there, unfastening her collar. Miss Gundry was teacher, colleague, and friend. She was sensible and kind, although matter-of-fact. But for the first time in years, she seemed a stranger.

"I'm not sure," answered Shizu quietly. "I haven't quite decided."

"But how can you hesitate?" cried Miss Gundry. "He seems like an unstable person."

"He has a great deal of initiative."

"But you heard him speak of gambling. And he's not a Christian."

"I could change all that," replied Shizu serenely. "I've always wanted to go to America."

Miss Gundry was visibly shocked, but she summoned a smile to her worried face and said gently. "Pray about it, dear." Bowing slightly, she left the room.

Shizu did pray, and think, and toss that night. But her last words to Tami kept returning to her mind.

"He seems so very nice."

CHAPTER FIVE

Third Class

They were married in a simple Friends' ceremony at the meetinghouse. Shizu wore an American wedding gown, and Chiyokichi striped trousers and a morning coat. Mr. Binford and Tami stood up with them.

The meetinghouse was full of Shizu's relatives, pupils, and friends. Mr. Miyamori and one of Chiyokichi's other friends were also present.

When everyone was seated, Chuzo Kaifu, head of the Friends School and Shizu's long time preceptor, arose. "I think now is the appropriate time," he said quietly, "for our young friends to pledge their vows."

Shizu and Chiyokichi stood facing the roomful of people. Shizu stretched out her right hand, and Chiyokichi took it. Shizu gave him a little glance that said, "Now!"

He spoke in Japanese. "In the presence of God and before these assembled friends, I take Shizuko Higuchi to be my wife, promising by Divine help to be unto her a loving and faithful husband as long as life shall last."

It was the time-honored Friends' ceremony, made familiar to Shizu through the journals of old Quaker stalwarts. As the waiting silence told Shizu it was her turn to repeat the vow, a picture came to her from the past. She remembered her first trip to Tokyo, and how her brother had compared it to a wedding journey. She felt near to Yataro as she spoke the solemn words. His spirit seemed to hover near her and admonish her to make a thrilling pilgrimage of this strange wedding journey she was just beginning.

As the new Mrs. Takahaski received the good wishes of her friends, she could see from anxious faces that in some cases they were indeed wishes rather than hopes. They liked Chiyokichi, but he was so different from Shizu—or perhaps it was just that he wasn't a Christian.

"You must be sure to look up the Naylors," they all said.

It was hardest, of course, to leave Tami.

"You must come to America, if we decide to stay. Try to join us, for the Higuchi relatives find it difficult to accept our Christian beliefs."

On Chiyokichi's advice, Shizu left her basket of family possessions. These were things that, as the oldest living child, she had received when her parents died. Old swords, the pride of her samurai forebears, and kimonos of rich fabric and exquisite pattern were among the precious treasures. There were also a few scrolls relating to famous incidents in Japanese history that Shizu's grandfather had received from Lord Hoshino. These were as highly prized for the beautiful brushwork of the written characters as they were valued for their historical significance.

"Leave the basket with your uncle; we can get the things when we come back," Chiyokichi suggested. "We have limited space for luggage."

She really didn't understand what he meant until they got to the pier.

"There's where you embark for first class," Shizu called, hurrying after her husband and striving to turn him in a different direction.

"Yes. But our passage is third class."

Third! Shizu came to an abrupt halt. All the missionaries she knew traveled first. She had never known anyone who traveled third class and she was unable to picture herself in such accommodations.

At that moment she remembered all the things her friends had tried to point out to her, which she had stubbornly ignored. The gambling, and the play-acting, and the vagueness about prospects. The nonchalance, and the different religion, and the giggle in prayer meeting.

"I—I don't think I'll go after all," she gasped. She turned half way around.

But it was too late. Her friends, down from Tokyo, waved encouragingly; the crowd pushed her on. And there stood Chiyokichi, waiting, with a look on his face that was wise, sad, merry, and understanding all at one time.

The anchor was aweigh; the ship was sailing. Yokohama slid away from them. The Pacific lay ahead—

and they were sailing east! Impertinently opposing the sun goddess, who always traveled from east to west.

Chiyokichi led her down to the third class quarters, to their tiny cabin below the water line. She could see why he had wanted her to leave the basket. They could scarcely get in the place together unless the door was closed.

"It's really not so bad here," he assured her. "There's company and it's always jolly. On my first trip I met sixteen young men from Kumamoto. They were really something to see. They were all dressed up in English hunting outfits—pink coats, breeches, boots, and all. Some tailor in Tokyo had told them that was the proper way to dress in the West!"

"Oh, my! Did you explain to them?" Shizu's quick concern took the edge off of Chiyokichi's tale. He himself had thought it a hilarious incident.

"I mentioned something about it, but they didn't believe me. I did enjoy disembarking with them. Watching people's faces, as those sixteen marched up Market Street!"

Shizu shook her head. "How embarrassed they must have been!"

Chiyokichi tipped up her face and looked into the serious eyes. "You are a wonder to me," he sighed. "More Japanese than I in some ways, despite your bringing-up. So tense and earnest. Can't you laugh a little? Let me tell you another story about my friends. When we reached Hawaii we were allowed to get off the boat and make some purchases. There were many unknown fruits, but I was cautious. I bought bananas, which I recognized. When we were back on board, I found these boys had been unable to resist two boxes of beautiful red fruit they'd never seen before. Someone told them they were tomatoes and you know we Japanese have always believed tomatoes to be poison! The boys just couldn't understand why anyone would be selling them, and boxed like that too."

"What did they do?"

"Threw them overboard," Chiyokichi answered, chuckling, "and watched me eat bananas."

"What a waste. I hope you shared your bananas with them."

As her husband had told Shizu, there were plenty of people around, and where there were people Chiyokichi always found friends. Soon he had discovered people who, like himself, were devotees of the theater.

A saké bottle was passed around and while Shizu sat stiffly watching, the men discussed their favorite plays. The talk got livelier and livelier, and one after another arose to act out his favorite role.

Shizu looked on with unwilling fascination. She'd never seen the Kabuki but she was familiar with some of the legends and characters that were re-enacted. These interpretations were even worse than she had imagined, although most of the humor was lost on her, as the men good-naturedly caricatured the melodramatic situations that were so familiar to them. The skill of her own husband, as he subtly mocked the conventions of the art, appalled her.

The fun grew broader and more hilarious. Shizu's own feelings of irritation mounted. As a Japanese wife she was ignored, but not for long. Finally the time came when she could sit still no longer.

She was small, and usually gentle, but now her spirit, shaped by the beliefs of her Quaker teachers, became a rod of tempered steel.

"Silence!" she cried. She didn't have to say it twice. It cut through the fun with the sharp edge of a samurai's sword. The men stopped and stared with amazement at the improbable spectacle the young Japanese wife was making. She didn't stop at their stares, but continued:

"You are vulgar and uncouth. This is a public place. Play acting is bad enough, but you are making it much worse. Be ashamed." She turned and walked away.

The next day there came an invitation from the captain. He had learned of the Takahashis from his friend, Inazo Nitobe, who had become a well known Japanese leader since the day Shizu had listened to him with such awe as he told her about Francis Xavier. The captain requested the young couple to join his table for dinner.

Chiyokichi went with Shizu, but declined subsequent invitations. He was happier with his relaxed Japanese-speaking friends. But Shizu, who had spent so many years in Christian schools, was happier visiting the captain and some missionaries and other Westerners.

Chiyokichi accepted this, as he accepted life in general, with broad tolerance. Perhaps, too, he was intrigued by the Western habits of his untypical Japanese wife. He welcomed her back and heard what she'd learned and whom she'd met.

On landing day they were up early like everyone else and poised eagerly at the rail.

Chiyokichi grew a little serious.

"There's one thing you must bear in mind. In the mission school, and on the ship, you are a special person, and the Westerners treat you as such. In California it's different. You'll be just another 'Jap.' "

"Oh, I know, the teachers often told me that the United States is not all Christian," Shizu answered. She looked out over the rail, and saw, materializing from sky and sea, the green hills and the tiny buildings of shining white cities. "How beautiful it is!"

They drew nearer, and the hills grew larger, and the watchers on shipboard were soon discovering the rocks, and cliffs, and then the commonplace paraphernalia of wharfs and docks. Shizu felt a little dazed. When they had landed and had boarded a streetcar to be taken to the ferry, she leaned close to her husband and whispered, "Everything's so large!"

The streets seemed wide and dirty. And she noticed that instead of the mere indifference to strangers that she had expected, there was a kind of sharp unfriendliness in some of the glances that fell on them.

On the ferry she forgot these things, for Oakland and Berkeley were so green and lovely—and then Chiyokichi pointed out the university.

"That's where I'll go some day!" she cried joyfully.

But as they drove through streets of jerry-built and

dingy buildings, she grew silent. Even the United States had its slums. And when the cab stopped and her husband opened the door, preparing to get out, Shizu was incredulous.

"Why are we getting out here?"

"This is my shop. Our home is right behind it."

Even Chiyokichi was depressed. During his absence the street seemed to have got dirtier, the shop smaller and dingier.

"Are all the shops like this in Oakland?" Shizu asked unbelievingly.

"Oh, no. There are streets of fine shops—many streets. And many blocks of lovely homes. But this is where the Japanese live and trade. This is our part of America."

Shizu surveyed the shop with its one treadle sewing machine, its kerosene lamps, and the cramped living quarters behind.

"I'll get in touch with the Naylors right away."

Shizu was not intending to accept this as her fate. There would be no shoving off of this Westernized daughter of a samurai into some unwanted corner. Her part of America, indeed!

And so the Takahashis, arriving in America one Saturday, in 1901, were at the Berkeley Friends Church the next day.

The Friends Church was not impressive. It was a little white frame building off in a hayfield. But waiting at the door was the warmly smiling minister, Mrs. Naylor. Her husband stood, solid and reassuring, behind her.

"Welcome! Welcome! We are so glad to see you!"

The Takahashis were invited to the Naylor home, a large and beautiful place with parqueted floors and marble fireplace. Young Mrs. Naylor, their daughter-in-law, asked Shizu to help her start a mother's club among the Japanese women.

"Oh, I should be glad to!" Shizu responded eagerly.

She had herself had the feeling when she arrived of being unwanted, an intruder. She realized now that her husband had lived a long time in the United States un-befriended. Most of the Japanese who came had no helpful connections, and above all didn't even know the language. They must all share this feeling of uneasiness.

Here was a place where Shizu could start her work.

They got settled in their home, such as it was. Mr. Naylor came to be measured for a suit, and others from the church followed him.

"Well, things are getting better already. I think it is all because I got married," Chiyokichi remarked gayly to his wife one day. "But I have never celebrated properly. I think I'll have a party soon, and ask my friends in to congratulate me."

Shizu tidied up the shop and cleaned house vigorously. Somehow it never really looked clean. She scrubbed the splintery floors and dusted the faded wall-paper, yearning for the familiar, translucent purity of Japanese *shōji* and the smooth integrity of polished wood.

She would prepare a real feast, she decided, for Chiyokichi's party. She had found some shops specializing in Japanese foodstuffs and had made her purchases with abandon, unmindful of her usual and necessary frugality. She stewed a chicken with fragrant black mushrooms and used some of the broth to make a clear soup in which she floated tiny flowers made from carrot slices. She crowned her work with a red snapper, care' fully cooked on slender bamboo supports, so that when done its head and tail turned up. Then she placed it on a nest of silvery white noodles, arranged to represent a fisherman's net. She was happy with the result—having lived so long in the mission school, she did not find it easy to make elaborate Japanese dishes.

Chiyokichi watched her preparations approvingly, closed the shop, and went out to make some purchases of his own. Shizu dreaded to see what he would bring, and yes, it was what she had feared, innumerable bottles of saké. Her heart was heavy, as she completed her tasks, the remembered mission warnings against alcohol ringing in her ears.

She met her husband's friends, and served the meal dutifully. But the men seemed a rough sort to her. It was the scene on the ship all over again. For a long while, Shizu sat quietly at one side and waited for it to be over, but the drinking and hilarity only increased as bottle after bottle joined the litter on the table.

The more she repressed her feelings as befitted a proper Japanese wife, the more intense her emotions became. Perhaps in later years the struggle between strong puri' tan values and Japanese tradition would produce less violent reactions as Shizu made peace with the duality that shaped her mind. Now however she rose, and with one imperious sweep of the arm, she flung all the bottles, full or empty, on the floor.

Then, as before, she silently retired.

An indignant clamor arose, punctuated here and there with Chiyokichi's amiable remarks as he tried to smooth over the situation. Before long, everyone was gone. Chiyokichi went to find his wife.

"They were drunk." She greeted her husband defiantly.

Chiyokichi shook his head. "They were celebrating my marriage. They were my friends. All I had."

"We have other friends now, who know how to live in a decent Christian way."

"I never heard you say that it was Christian to be rude—to insult one's friends. Some were my customers, too. They will not forget easily. How shall we live if we antagonize our neighbors?"

"Many more Japanese are coming to the United States," Shizu replied firmly.

She was right about the immigrants, though this was not a mass immigration, numbering thousands by the month, such as the United States had often known. The year 1900 had been the peak, with over twelve thousand Japanese coming to the United States. Although the rate slackened, a good many came yearly until 1909.

Shizu's hospitality, although not convivial in Chiyokichi's way, was just as spontaneous. "Let's have *gochiso*," was a recurring phrase in the household as Shizu proposed a dinner for one or another new arrival. She would have liked to welcome them all.

"Let's invite the family that moved in over the photo-graphic shop," she remarked one day. "And Mr. Na-kano and the Fujimotos."

"Good, good, and I'll cook the dinner," agreed Chiyokichi.

He had learned during his theatrical years to cook ex-tremely well. He was particularly proud of his *teriyaki*. True, nearly every family broiled their chicken or fish in this traditional manner, but the success of the dish de-pended upon the marinade. Chiyokichi had developed his to perfection—soy sauce and honey, not sugar, to the proper proportions, a bit of fresh ginger and—this was his secret—a whiff of garlic.

"I'll fix *teriyaki* and . . ."

After they had eaten, the guests began to tell their stories. They had launched out, like all immigrants, into the bright new world to seek a home, adventure, or just simply to seek their fortune. The Fujimotos had tried Hawaii first, but there high prices swallowed the high wages, and plantation conditions smothered both prog-ress and the hope of it.

Now they had come to California, lured by the labor contractors who made even brighter promises for the mainland.

"And what do we find where ever we go?" Mr. Fuji-moto was plaintive. "These big signs that say, 'No Japa-nese allowed!'"

Chiyokichi tried to answer. "I read a lot about it in the Japanese papers. The big growers need lots of labor, because they have such big farms. It's almost like the *daimyo* in Japan, before their fiefs were broken up. But in the small towns . . ."

"Here," Mr. Ono interrupted, "the lords of the land owe no duty to the farm workers, as in Japan. The workers are always fearful that they'll lose their place and work, and so they are suspicious of outsiders like us."

Mr. Ono was the new neighbor from above the photographic shop. A vigorous man, he was outspoken in his anger and disappointment.

"Did you hear," said Mr. Nakano, who had been in the United States longer than the rest, "about the bubonic plague quarantine? They isolated all the Japanese and Chinese in San Francisco."

Chiyokichi nodded. "The plague was nothing but gossip . . ."

Shizu, sitting with the women, had been watching for an opportunity to draw the group together so she could invite them all to church. Only half-hearing, she seized on her husband's words.

"Nothing but gossip," she repeated. "This talk is getting you nowhere. You can do nothing to improve your lot until you know the language. There is an English class every week at my friend Mrs. Naylor's house. Don't you want to come, Mrs. Fujimoto, Mrs. Ono? And then you can teach your husbands at night. I would also like to invite you all to our church."

"What kind of church? I am a Buddhist," answered Mr. Ono. "I don't know why we Japanese should have to take up the foreign religion."

"Christianity is not a foreign religion," said Shizu. It was her opening for a little sermon, and Shizu was eloquent. When she was through, she taught them all a hymn—her favorite—"What a Friend We Have in Jesus."

When Shizu's guests went away, she hoped that they no longer felt wholly like strangers.

This went on week after week, and the English classes, the Bible classes, and Shizu's Japanese Mother's Club grew and grew. A good many Japanese came as members to the Friends Church, and many more went on to other cities or towns or fields with increased hope and courage.

Shizu learned there was one personal hope she must defer. The lovely university in Berkeley was waiting for her, but she couldn't answer its call just yet. There wasn't money, in the first place. In the second, she was going to have a baby—of course, it would be a boy.

"His last name should be Higuchi," Shizu asserted.

She was severe, because her husband had declined at marriage to follow her uncle's suggestion that he take the Higuchi name. It was a custom in Japan for families who had no sons to adopt a son-in-law, so that the name would be carried on. Shizu frequently pointed out that Chiyokichi had plenty of brothers to carry on *his* name.

"You want this son to worship your ancestors at the Shinto shrine, or the Buddhist?" inquired Chiyokichi. "If you want either one, I'll let you name him Higuchi!"

"All right," acquiesced Shizu. "Takahashi he remains. He could have carried on a noble name. Anyway, for an

American first name, I should like to call him George."

"After George Fox?" Chiyokichi had learned all about Shizu's heroes.

"Could there be a better person to name him after?"

"George Washington," retorted Chiyokichi, remembering that a number of his Japanese friends had named their first-born sons for America's hero.

The baby came. It was a boy, the most wonderful of all boys. Now they were mother, father, son. Shizu's own family had been scattered for so long that it was wonderful, this warm family feeling.

"I want a lot of children, so they won't be lonely," she told her husband, looking down contentedly at the sleeping child.

"You want that more than going to the university? More than teaching, speaking to large groups, and doing important things?" Chiyokichi knew her well by now.

"If I have many children they can help the world a lot more than just me," said Shizu. "Besides, I'll do all those other things, too!"

CHAPTER SIX

The Inner Light

Chiyokichi, trying to improve his business prospects, decided to move to Berkeley. But hunting a location was discouraging. Shizu kept hoping they could move near the church. Once they thought they had found just the place, only to be turned down because they were Japanese. They finally found a place on Shattuck Avenue. It was really more than Chiyokichi had planned to pay, but he felt they had to take it.

The years sped by. George was soon joined by Henry, then by William. Little sisters, too, started arriving. They were welcome, for Chiyokichi and Shizu both wanted a big family, but it was becoming increasingly hard to find the money for their support.

Chiyokichi was tireless and full of ingenuity. He learned hat-blocking from a hatter near him on Shattuck Avenue, and later gave lessons in the art. He became an expert shopper, learning all about bargains and buying to advantage for his growing family. He told Shizu about his exploits, and she listened with wonder.

"I know nothing about money," she would say.

Chiyokichi knew this to be true. Between the samurai principles—that held money concerns to be ignoble—and missionary teaching—that God would provide—Shizu had grown up without her husand's capacity for practicality.

Chiyokichi had not only become a good shopper but he had grown in other ways, too. He had long since given up the amusements Shizu found so trying, and finally he joined the warm fellowship of the church, although he was not, like his wife, a constant attendant. The English language had never opened to him enough to let him fully participate. He was a "strong, silent pillar." But he heard from his wife all that went on.

In time, the Friends decided they were outgrowing their little church, and with banker Naylor's support, they made plans to build a new one. Chiyokichi learned this bit of news from his wife with an unexpectedly lively interest.

"Now, I wonder," he murmured. He took a look at the old church, walking around and around it with more than devotional attention. "They've raised the rent in Shattuck Avenue, and it's too crowded for us, anyway. There's the manse beside the church—we could live there while I remodeled the church. Plenty of room."

He paid a visit to Mr. Naylor, whose benevolent bent in many instances opened the way or saved the day. When Chiyokichi went home, he announced to Shizu that he had bought the church, for their new home and shop.

Shizu welcomed the idea, and though she had begun

to be troubled by asthma, she embarked on the hard work of moving to Haste Street without delay.

But moving didn't end their troubles. One can't take care of six or seven people with what would barely stretch for three or four.

The milkman knocked at the door one morning when he brought the milk.

"This is the last order I can bring till the bill is paid."

Shizu looked at him hopelessly. "But the children need milk to drink!"

"So do mine," said the milkman, with that blank glance Shizu had learned to dread. *You have no right to be here anyway, taking up room in our country.* The look was usually covered up, but at a time like this, at any crisis, it could glare suddenly out of faces you had thought were those of friends.

And then the gas man came with a big wrench to shut off the gas.

The chill of winter was in the air that day and it seemed to grip Shizu's chest with an insistent tightness. She wheezed and gasped as she fought for air and finally she sank down in a chair and desultorily watched the children playing with their blocks. Their growing life relentlessly demanded milk, heat, food and clean clothes. How was she to manage everything? The dreadful pressure in her chest would surely strangle her. Dirty dishes in the sink; the morning's wash in the basket; little food in the cupboard. And she couldn't move—in fact, she could scarcely breathe. Her thoughts drifted back to Japan.

On an evening when the spring mists
Trail over the wide sea,
And sad is the voice of the cranes
I think of my far-off home.

Thinking of home,
Sleepless I sit,
The cranes call amid the shore reeds,
Lost in the mists of spring.[1]

Japan—where others cared for the children, and a lady could read poety and write it, too, and could practice the art of calligraphy, which Shizu loved. She remembered the missionaries, who, loving hard work, yet could choose the work that interested them, and delegate the dishwashing and scrubbing. Oh, this was a hard life she had chosen—not the life she'd meant to live at all!

The baby whimpered, and Shizu managed to get to the crib and pick her up. She was a round, sweet, black-eyed baby, gurgling when she saw her mother. Sharper agony than asthma or self-pity pierced Shizu's breast. No harm must come to her babies. The babies must have milk and heat and light. But how?

Suddenly the front door banged, and little George came running in. "Mother, look what Mrs. Kawamura just gave me!"

It was a beautiful big apple.

"Divide it up, Mother," said George, dancing with

[1] From the Man'yoshu. In *Anthology of Japanese Literature*, ed. by Donald Keene, New York, Grove Press, 1955. Used by permission.

eagerness. "So Henry and William and you can have some, too."

Shizu took the apple to the kitchen, cut it, and then stared at the pieces. "Oh, dear, I've made a mistake. I've cut three pieces instead of four. Never mind, I don't need one; there are enough for you boys."

George looked distressed. Then his face cleared. "Oh, that's all right, Mother, you eat the third one. I don't care." And he ran off cheerfully to join his younger brothers in their game.

Shizu looked after him. Her depression lifted. Why, this was what life really was, the loving and giving spirit that God had put in little George—and in all men.

> From plum-scented veil
> Of haze, suddenly rose the sun
> On the mountain trail.

Her breathing seemed to ease, and soon she was able to get to work again, using the hand washing machine that had been such a novelty to their Japanese friends when her husband had first brought it home.

Chiyokichi came from the shop a little early. "Oi, oi," he called.

Shizu tried to hold on to her new-found serenity. There was nothing wrong in calling "Oi," it was just "Hi!", or "Hey!" It was only that missionaries had been more dignified in addressing their wives. Chiyokichi knew Shizu didn't quite like it, and did it half to tease.

"Yes," she answered calmly. She must give him strength. She must not tell him yet about the milk and the gas; she would wait till he was fed and rested. But what could she have for dinner?

"See!" Chiyokichi cried, coming in and waving a package in the air. "Chickens! We'll have a feast."

He went on into the kitchen while she stared. "I also paid the milkman and the gas company. That man who left the suit at the shop since way last summer—I thought he would never come and get it—came in to-day, and paid me, and ordered another, and gave me something in advance."

"Chicken! Chicken!" shouted the children, scampering into the kitchen to watch with fascination as their father prepared the unexpected feast.

"And after dinner we will roast chestnuts!" their father exclaimed. "And then tell stories!"

Shizu watched with smiling eyes. She was greatly relieved that Chiyokichi had been able to pay the bills. She was warmed by his gaiety. But she was glad that first she had been able to discover help within.

CHAPTER SEVEN

An Episode of Cherries

Help within, the Inner Light, had sustained Shizu through many years, and Chiyokichi, too, had drawn his strength from hers, but sometimes he jested about her faith—like this morning.

Shizu was pleased when her husband came early to his breakfast tea.

"Would it be all right if I went out to a meeting to' night?" she asked as she set before him his dish of rice gruel.

"Does the wind ask the mountain if it may blow?" inquired her husband.

Shizu eyed him quickly.

But her husband's eye narrowed in his irresistible smile, and Shizu, relieved, smiled too.

"It's all right, then? I'll have to see if my shoes are still presentable. Will you come to the meeting with me?"

"What kind of meeting is it? A church meeting at which you interpret the long sermons according to the Inner Light, making them better than they were to be'

gin with?" Chiyokichi made a long face, in mock seri-
ousness.

"No," she answered, pained at his jesting. "This is to
hear a speaker from Japan, Toyohiko Kagawa. He
preaches in a terrible slum in Kobe. He has decided it is
necessary to do more than preach to the poor, or give
charity; he advocates a new form of trade called cooper-
atives. He is now helping Sakai-san to form a cooperative in the Coachella Valley."

"Ah, the onion growers!" exclaimed Chiyokichi. A
farmer's son, he kept a lively interest in agriculture.
"Those fellows who lived through the heat and near-
starvation, and finally found that onions would grow
in the sand and could be cropped early—well, they deserve the high prices they're getting! It's back-breaking
work putting out the sets, one by one."

"Now they're sending for their wives and families,
and Dr. Kagawa is helping Sakai-san set up a regular
Christian community there."

"If you have seed, and water, and earth, and enough
care, you can produce growth," said Chiyokichi seriously. "This is the deepest fact of life."

Shizu answered like a flash, in a *haiku* made for the
occasion:

> *Earth, and rain, and care—*
> *But in the seed, life, which must*
> *Be already there.*

The door banged open. "Is breakfast ready?"
It was George, dressed for school, his hair parted a

little crooked and smacked down. "Oh, gee, nothing but *o-kai* again!"

"You must not say gee," said his mother firmly. "*O-kai* is nourishing."

But she sighed. She would have liked so much to give the children something more substantial for breakfast than thin rice gruel. But *o-kai* filled them up, and soon, surely, things would grow a little better.

She went to the meeting (after carefully blacking the shoes she saved to wear when interpreting) and was en- thralled by the visions of Dr. Kagawa that stretched into eternity—but began right next door. The cooperative in the Coachella Valley was organized very practically, and promised well. It was to divide its profits three ways, one third for the church, one third for the lan- guage school, and the other third for its own mainte- nance and improvement. Dr. Kagawa told Shizu after- ward of his work in Japan, and his connections with some of the Christians Shizu knew best. Her contact with him strengthened her sense of participation in the continuing work in Japan.

One of her ties with Japan, however, had been broken —but happily, for Tami had now joined her in America, just as Shizu had hoped years before. And what a joy it had been to take part in her sister's wedding, a real white-gown American wedding in the Berkeley Friends Church! Perhaps, Shizu thought to herself, hopefully, perhaps it was the first such Japanese wedding in Amer- ica.

Yet no matter how much interested Shizu was in

Japan and her old friends, it was secondary to the life she was living in America.

Spring had come late, but at last Berkeley's hills were a tender green, drifted with white cherry blossoms that gave out a fragrance unknown to the rosy Japanese trees.

"Mother!" shouted one of the boys, rushing in from Sunday school. "I am going to be a Buddhist." He threw down a very small Easter basket in childish disgust.

Shizu gazed at him, too horrified to speak.

"Well—at least a Methodist," he amended. "The Buddhists' Easter baskets are biggest, but even the Methodists' are bigger than ours."

Shizu searched for English words. The Buddhists shouldn't have Easter baskets—they'd just copied the Christian Sunday schools. Naturally, they would make them bigger! But why Easter baskets anyway?

The little girls came in before she had time to answer her son. They carried their baskets calmly, content in their bright cerise dresses. They had always worn starched white, but had got so tired of it that Chiye, who was always having ideas, thought of dyeing the old dresses, and now they seemed like new.

But when Chiye tried to put a matching ribbon in her hair, Shizu said, "No." She had thoroughly absorbed Quaker ideas of plainness, which were not uncongenial to her background. Samurai families had been allowed to use and wear fine objects not permitted other classes, but philosophically they eschewed luxury and display, believing in plain living and high thinking.

No ribbon!

The girls, however, had a champion in Chiyokichi, who took over here, too, going shopping with them when Shizu was sick just as he went shopping for food and household necessities.

It was he who bought Chiye and Michi a little hand sewing machine for making doll clothes, and later a big sewing machine to make their own clothes. He helped them buy material, too—in the bright, gay colors they loved. He understood, of course, all about sewing and taught Chiye, and although they bought patterns, Chiye soon learned to adapt them to suit herself. She would change the sleeves, or skirt, or collar, and always put a little embroidery here or there.

The children worked hard. The boys had paper routes and errands to run after school—or after language school to which they sometimes went. The girls hurried home to help with the washing, ironing, cleaning, or else to mind the babies. Sometimes one or another had to stay home from school to help because Shizu was down with asthma.

The years were happy years, though, and the children managed to have lots of fun together. And there was plenty of room for all kinds of adventure. The old church building on Haste Street had changed indeed since the Takahashi family had moved there.

At the time of the San Francisco Chinatown fire, Chiyokichi had bought up loads of salvaged lumber. He hired a carpenter, and put up a store on the front of the lot. He added rooms to the church, built a hothouse, as well as some apartments, and erected an office building that was rented by the Japanese Association.

Between the church-house and the buildings along the street was an empty space, a sort of court. Here Chiyokichi made a garden, with trees and shrubs, a tea-house, and a double pond with a bridge.

The children played all kinds of games in the garden. Sometimes they even played school in the teahouse, where there was a Liberty Bell that they used for a school bell. On Saturday afternoons they went on pic-nics to the big hilly campus of the University of Cali-fornia. Occasionally they brought back minnows from their Saturday outings. Then they would make their own miniature gardens with ponds and bridges. The girls had fun, too, experimenting with baking, which Shizu had never mastered.

The boys' fun was not always so circumspect. They learned to get out a bedroom window by a rope, so their departures could be made without inconvenient explana-tions.

One day a neighbor came to the front door and rang.

Shizu answered, and cordially invited him to enter, although she had a dozen shirts and dresses dampened in the laundry basket. She liked guests, and always pre-ferred conversation to ironing.

This guest, however, appeared uncomfortable. He sat down, but kept turning a cap over and over in his hands. A rather small cap. A cap that looked familiar.

"Why, George must have lost his cap!" cried Shizu. "He's a heedless boy."

She held out her hand for it.

"So it is George's cap?" said the neighbor. "Well, I found it under my cherry tree—and all the cherries gone."

He got up and departed, while Shizu stood speechless with the cap in her hands.

She went back to her ironing, and while she ironed, her thoughts went round and round.

"It can't be that George would do such a thing! He has always been such a good boy."

But the cap! The evidence was pretty clear.

"How could he steal our neighbor's cherries! Maybe he has bad tendencies!" Her heart ached. "How have I failed? What have I done wrong? I must have done something so wrong."

When George got home from school, the shirts and dresses hung from the chandelier, smooth and crisp and faintly smelling of starch. But Shizu sat waiting in the parlor. Not rocking the baby. Not reading. There was something strange in this. George paused, a little chilled.

"George, will you come with me."

George followed her into her bedroom. She closed the door.

"Sit down, please, George."

George sat down stiffly, his heart beating on his ribs.

His mother went to her dresser and picked up the cap. Like a flash, understanding smote George.

With the cap in her hands, Shizu sat down opposite him. She bowed her head. "Dear God, forgive me. Somehow I have made a mistake. My little boy has stolen.

I was wrong. I taught him wrong. Dear God, forgive me."

Shizu's voice broke. It was a voice that had always spoken to George calmly and lovingly. Once in a while sternly. But George had never before heard it trembling with sorrow.

"Oh, Mama, Mama, I did steal the cherries," George wailed, falling to the floor beside her knees. "Oh, Mama, Mama, it wasn't your fault. I'll be good. I'll always be good from now on."

Then they prayed together. George was sure he'd never do wrong again.

But sometimes wrong wore such attractive disguises. It was such fun, for instance, to roller-skate, only the days didn't hold hours enough—after language school, and jobs, and study. The boys had discovered a street of smooth sidewalks, a long, long hill to swoop down at breakneck speed, but dinnertime always came much too soon.

"Let's go out again after dinner," one of the boys suggested as they put their skates away.

"Can't. Mama'd never let us."

"Well, we can let down that rope from the window. Come on."

It wasn't as if they were really doing anything wrong. It wasn't like the cherries, George thought. The boys found that it was even more fun at night than in the daytime. Their exuberant joy in the long swift flight to the bottom of the hill found expression in wild cries. They didn't give a thought to the neighbors on each side of the street, some of them trying to sleep behind open windows.

"It's really getting late. We'd better get home," George, his conscience suddenly coming alive, bethought himself.

They rushed home and quickly shinnied up the rope. They dived into bed. Just then the doorbell rang.

George crept to the place where you could hear what went on in the living-room.

"Yes? Why, how do you do! It's Officer O'Brien, isn't it?" George heard his mother say cordially.

"Yes, Ma'am, and I want to know where your boys are, Ma'am!"

"My boys?" repeated Shizu with some pride. "They are in bed."

"Well, we had complaints from over on the avenue, that some kids was roller-skating up and down the hill and raising Ned with their yelling and all. Somebody thought it was your kids. Sure they're in bed? Sure they been there all evening?"

"I am perfectly sure."

"Oh, well, then, sorry, Ma'am. I'm—I'm real sorry. I beg your pardon. We have to look into these complaints, you know."

George crept back to bed. What should he do now? Confess all? No, never, because then his mother would consider that she'd told a lie, and that, added to her sorrow over the sins of her boys, would be almost more than she could bear. In all kindness, George assured himself, he must not tell her.

But he wasn't sure she wouldn't find out just from looking at his face. He kept his eyes on his food for several meals.

For George had come to the considered conviction that his mother knew everything—just like God.

George was a great reader, and his mind was eager and acquisitive. Each new fact was like a valued possession, or rather, like a projection of himself into new territory, and each bit of knowledge he hurried to share with his mother.

She was always receptive, showing pleasure over each discovery he made. But it was a recognizing pleasure—these were things she seemed to know already. George couldn't figure it out. Of course, she was always reading, he knew that—sitting with the baby carriage beside her, shaking it with her foot while she read. Gasping for breath with asthma, she still managed to read. But after all, how could a person remember all the details of American history like that, and science, and English grammar? She knew all about Japanese history, too, and tried to teach them in the summer, though they weren't much interested.

What George didn't know was that after he was in bed, and everybody was asleep, and the house was quiet, his mother would steal out and find his books, wrap up warmly, pull up a chair under the light, and do her son's assignment.

Shizu wanted to understand the culture that was shaping her children. She wanted to be able to help them; to know what was happening to their minds.

Perhaps, too, it was that learning itself was irresistible to her.

While Shizu was busy with the children's welfare from the inside out, Chiyokichi was tirelessly working and building. He was renting his new apartments now not only to newcomers from Japan, but sometimes to old acquaintances who had been driven out of agriculture.

The Fujimotos came back. They were deeply discouraged. They had worked hard, and they had done well, at first.

"The first day, I was so surprised. They told me to go home before noon," Mr. Fujimoto reminisced. "I had been working hard and had already done the whole day's work. We all kept working hard, though, and pretty soon we rose from being day laborers to being tenant farmers."

"Still we worked," Mrs. Fujimoto sighed. "The whole family, even the children, except when they were in school. We saved, and saved, and we were all ready to buy a farm—when this law passed."

She spoke of the California Alien Land Law of 1913. This prevented "aliens ineligible to citizenship" from buying land, and restricted them to three-year leases.

"You didn't want to lease?" Chiyokichi asked them.

"For three years, not knowing if your lease would be renewed?" answered Mr. Fujimoto. "Maybe they'll pass another law to prevent even the leasing. No, I'd rather open a little shop, here among the Japanese, and not try farming any more."

Many sad and discouraged people came to the Taka-hashis' home for help and comfort, which they received in different ways. They ate Chiyokichi's delicious meals, and sang hymns with the family, and drew cheer from Shizu's hopeful spirit.

Chiyokichi entertained them all, guests and family. Fairy tales, like "Urashima and the Tongue-Cut Sparrow," gave way as the children grew older to *Chushin-Gura,* a play about forty-seven *ronin,* knights errant, who spent two years preparing vengeance for their master's slayer, and then surrendered to justice; the story of Benkei, who stole the temple bell of Mii and lugged it back to his own gang of warrior monks, only to become so angry when it whimpered "Take me back to Mii Temple," that he kicked it all the way back. Story after story, from old plays and legends full of pageantry and ancient poetry and wisdom, were retold by Chiyo-kichi, whose dramatic flair remained untouched by time.

CHAPTER EIGHT

Beginning Tensions

The Court of the Universe, the Tower of Jewels, the Court of the Four Seasons, the Mosque of Sultan Ahmen I, and Kyoto's Golden Pavilion, Kinkaku, and the Zone, with its ten million dollars' worth of amusement concessions—all of them, and more, were a part of that wondrous spectacle, the Panama-Pacific International Exposition of 1915.

For the few months of the exposition, the carnival spirit swept away the fog of nativist fears and hostilities that had harrassed Orientals for so long, leaving the beauty of the bay cities and their peoples shining in the sun.

Of course, it was hard work and trouble for those grown-up and efficient people who have to manage fairs. But for the children and the young in heart, it was bustle, and glamor, and a sense of possibilities.

The Takahashis' lively faculties were thoroughly mobilized. Chiyokichi had looked about and assessed the opportunities. Space. He still had space, and there would be innumerable visitors. He could provide housing!

So a second story was made in the church by cutting off the lofty ceiling space of the old "dormitory," and the new floor was subdivided for apartments.

What else could he do? A concession? Chiyokichi racked his brains. Some kind of concession. What kind?

"I'll make pancakes," he decided. "I make good pancakes."

The only trouble was, someone else had already arranged to make pancakes, and no rival concessions were allowed by the Exposition Committee.

Chiyokichi was undaunted. "I'll make rice-flour pancakes," he told the committee. (To this day his children aren't sure how much rice-flour went into those pancakes. The rice-flour sack was in evidence, surely.)

So the family had not only the opportunity to visit the collected glories of the world, but they had the fun of being a working part of the spectacle. They knew its structure and its people, and they made friends—a famous opera singer, a statesman, many another interesting person.

One of the great pleasures Chiyokichi drew from the exposition was to roam around the Court of Flowers and the Court of Palms and the Palace of Horticulture. He especially enjoyed the collection of *bonsai*. These tiny dwarfed trees, the result of thousands of years of study and practice, fascinated his children, too, but they were content to look and pass on to something else.

Chiyokichi stayed, talked with the horticulturists from Japan, who grew and trained the trees, and finally bought some *hego,* the dried tree-fern from Hawaii in which the little trees were grown.

The fair was over, and it had been a rich experience. But the Takahashis' apartments hadn't rented as well as had been hoped, and a new burden of debt was put on Chiyokichi's small but sturdy shoulders.

The fair was over, but new excitement exploded in California, as the United States entered the first world war. It seemed as though this threat of common danger drew the varied people of the state together. Japan had entered the war on the side of the Allies only fifteen days after England's opening of hostilities. The move was not really popular in Japan, where admiration of Germany was general. Japan's decision was, indeed, the result of an alliance of two dissimilar groups: the inter-nationalists, to whom the Anglo-Japanese Alliance seemed binding, and the militarists, who welcomed the chance to seize Germany's Asian colonies.

At any rate, Japan's action in joining the Allies temporarily improved the situation for the issei, Japanese nationals in America, who had been unable to apply for citizenship, and for their American-born children, the nisei.

Perhaps the admiration won by the beautiful Japanese exhibits at the exposition helped. And no doubt the increased need for Japanese labor on the farms contributed to the new acceptance.

While tension eased for a time between the races, a new one was developing within most Japanese-American families. The issei had made their adjustment to life in California by becoming self-sufficient. Practically, it was all they could do. Walled off from the life of the new country, they perpetuated the old. They rebuilt Japan in their homes and in their segregated communities, and enjoyed for a while a false security.

Their children, however, the nisei, were growing up. They'd been born in this country. They'd gone to its schools. With the heart-warming, heart-aching hopefulness of youth, they had made advances to the society that shut out their parents, advances that youth on the other side could not and did not repel. The customs of old Japan, unquestioning filial obedience, repression of individual differences, and the subordination of the person to the group, began to lose hold on the children, and the parents were naturally frightened and sad, and some even angered.

The Takahashi home was not typical. Yet, even here, there were strains, although the rebellion was not as much against Japanese, as against religious, restraints.

One Sunday morning, Shizu happened to come down a little early to start getting breakfast. She surprised her second son Henry with his hand on the doorknob.

"What! Where are you going? It's too early for Sunday school."

Then she noticed how he was dressed.

"You were sneaking away to play football!"

Henry moved his weight from one foot to the other.

"Well—I know how you feel about football on Sunday, but this time—you see, I'm the quarterback. They need me. Without me, they'll lose."

"Does it make it any less Sunday?"

"But a person should do what he can for his team!"

"No team is worth while unless God's on it, too." Shizu looked at him in wistful perplexity. "How is it you don't understand that? I haven't done right, oh, I haven't done right."

Henry went back on the other foot and relinquished all hope for the game. All he hoped was . . .

"Come here, dear, we'll take it to God." At Shizu's words, Henry knew he was lost.

The children never seemed to resent these prayer sessions. Shizu was so humble, loving, and troubled. She didn't invoke God against them, or even ask him to be on her side. She just asked for help. And as far as the children could see, she certainly got it!

Once Ernie, one of the little brothers, felt the effect of one of these sessions after Sunday Meeting. They sat there in rows, as usual—but it was such a temptation to get up a silent communion of eyes during the long, sober Meeting.

Grandma Naylor was speaking. Now retired, she had been the pastor when the Takahashis first came, and through all the long years she had been a constant help and friend in time of trouble. The children well knew that they couldn't be unruly when Grandma Naylor was speaking.

One absolutely daren't giggle, thought Ernie, repressing a surge of mirth as he glanced down the row of profiles beside him. They all looked so funny, each nose pointing just a little differently, a slight degree more up or down. And then, Willy caught his eye, and a spark of laughter jumped from one to the other. Ernie grabbed for his handkerchief. He'd stuff up his mouth, then he just couldn't giggle.

He stuffed and stuffed, and suddenly stuffed it too far. His throat rebelled and he choked. Oh, what a choke, a momentous, a record-breaking choke! Whole rows of Takahashi morale broke down simultaneously.

All Ernie could do was to hope against hope that his father would spank him. His father had a big ring that could make quite a dent, but nothing one couldn't get over. When Ernie saw Shizu's face after Meeting, he knew he was doomed. She was looking determined and sad all at once, and when they got home, she led him off and prayed with him just as he feared she would.

Shizu's prayer sessions never inhibited her big fun-loving family for long. There was always something new to play, something to do.

The boys loved football. Tickets were too high for them to go to the games very often, but this didn't deter them. The Berkeley terrain provided certain natural advantages—the boys could see the college playing field from the hillside just above the stadium.

Shizu never went to the games but she would urge Chiyokichi to take the family.

Everyone would get excited and jump up and wave his arms and yell, and have a wonderful time. Somehow one day Chiyokichi lost his footing and slid all the way down the hill into the top row of benches. He ended up sitting on a lady's lap.

He got up right away and apologized, smiling and bowing politely, but the lady's husband got mad. Chiyo-kichi tried to calm him down with a joke, but it didn't work very well.

The family didn't get to see the end of that game, and afterwards they either bought tickets or stayed home.

The first world war ended and a new era began—the promised time of freedom and democracy. Ordinary activities were resumed, and Shizu was again in demand for interpreting, although she could but seldom get away from home. At various meetings, where famous men and imposing women were inclined to overlook her at the beginning, she became the center of attention after the program. Whether she changed the speech from English to Japanese, or Japanese to English, she could preserve, or even enhance, its meaning by her clear and eloquent language.

Seiju Hirakawa, who had succeeded Chuzo Kaifu as principal of the Girls' School, visited America, and Shizu learned at first hand of the continuing growth and service of her school. She heard how her old friend, Gurney Binford, and his wife and others had been working with Kagawa-san in forming New Life Societies, training young men to go back to their villages and work for a more abundant life for the villagers. They used the same plan Kagawa had followed in helping the onion growers to start a cooperative in Coachella Valley. They always started by helping people; teaching them better ways of planting and harvesting, introducing new seeds, teaching them how to improve their communities, their homes. Then, when the people asked, "Why do you take all this trouble for us?" they would give them the answer.

Shizu learned from many people of other Christian work in Japan—the manifold, widespread effort, of which the Friends' projects were only a small part of the vigorous whole.

Shizu's children became rather tired of missionaries' visits. Dressed in their neat best, they were always expected to show up as worthy offspring of their illustrious mother. They handed round cookies at tea, wore pasted-on smiles, and wished over and over again that they were elsewhere. Out of all this onerous routine, one visit was memorable for its fun. Shizu was entertaining a voluble religious guest. Tea was poured, and the guest talked. Cookies were passed, and she talked. She seemed oblivious to all that went on, except her own words. One of the boys decided to test this assumption —the lady's pious left hand held a cookie, while the other described geometrical motions to illustrate what she was saying. Suddenly the cookie disappeared.

The lady looked round, but only the blandest of serious faces looked back. Perhaps she believed she had eaten the cookie. She took another and launched out on another long tale. Again the cookie disappeared. Could they dare try it again?

Whether she ever caught on or not, the children never knew. But at least, in this case they felt avenged.

As they grew older, they did wish their mother were not quite so universal in her religious interest. Some of them had to go with her to witness the wonders performed by Aimee Semple McPherson.

"But she's not a Quaker," they objected, dragging their heels.

"She's a Christian," their mother replied firmly, "and she's trying harder than some Quakers to do what Christ taught. Jesus accomplished faith healing on a good many occasions. If you have faith like a mustard seed, you can move mountains."

"Then I wish someone would move V. S. McClatchy and the Oriental Exclusion League right out into the Pacific Ocean," muttered one of the boys, who had been reading a series of articles just starting in the *Sacramento Bee*.

These articles were to herald a vague but virulent crusade against the Japanese. "They're taking jobs that belong to us—they're trying to get our land" were some of the mildest of the accusations. Planned political campaigns exploited the animosities, and near-violence flared from time to time. But even when a new California land law was passed, in 1920, Shizu tried to be philosophical. Ineligible aliens could no longer even lease the land they farmed, just as Mr. Fujimoto had feared. Nor could they own stock in land corporations. And to prevent their buying in the names of their minor children who were, of course, citizens, parents were declared ineligible as legal guardians of children who owned real property.

"God will take care of all these things, in his good time," Shizu assured her family. "Besides, we're not the only ones having trouble right now. I've been reading in the newspapers. There was a mobbing of Italians in a town in Illinois the other day. And have you heard of this Ku Klux Klan?"

"God works in a mysterious way," her son jested, quoting his mother's oft-repeated phrase.

"It's all the spirit that comes after a war," Shizu continued soberly, ignoring her son's lighthearted remark.

The brothers looked at each other. "That's very much what our Y leader was saying the other day. Frustration and disillusionment. Depression and lawlessness. The effort of the hundred-per-centers to lay the blame for all these troubles on people outside their own group. It's funny how often Mom comes up with the right answer. Coincidental, huh, Mom?"

"It's not coincidental at all," Shizu retorted. "It's the way things work in God's universe."

CHAPTER NINE

And One Blossom More

The children were growing up. There were twelve of them now, evenly divided, six boys and six girls. From lovable babies, and mischievous children, they were all changing into self-willed teen-agers. Shizu often invoked the spirit of Elizabeth Fry, who had also despaired about her lively brood:

"I desire to examine where I can mend towards my beloved little ones," confessed Mrs. Fry in her journal, "but it is not in my power to turn them or alter their motives, but I must in humility endeavor to do my best." [1]

Added concerns were not all, however, that accompanied the children's growing up. Shizu discovered that she once again had a little, just a little time for herself.

For years the teachers had been eager to enlist her in P.T.A. Now she could attend meetings, and even take office. The three great principles that had animated the W.C.T.U. at its beginning in Japan in 1886—World Prohibition, World Peace, and World Purity—still

[1] Memoirs of the Life of Elizabeth Fry.

called clearly to Shizu, and she joined this organization. In time she became the district president, and had the joy of celebrating the apparent victory of Prohibition. As the children began to reach university age, she joined the University of California's Mother's Club—the first Japanese. She treasured this membership, for it represented the attainment by her children of her own long-held hopes for a college education.

The older children had become interested in a new organization, the Young People's Christian Conference of Northern California, which Henry had helped to start.

This was not at Shizu's behest. She had vowed to keep her children in church until they were through high school, but after that she and Chiyokichi felt they should be able to use their own judgment. This Christian work of Henry and the others sustained their most hopeful convictions.

The Young People's Christian Conference held monthly meetings at the Congregational church. Shizu often visited and listened to their discussions of religion, discussions couched in different phrases from those so long familiar to her. And yet the idea struck a deep chord of understanding.

The young people discovered Jesus' peace imperative as though for the first time, and Shizu remembered her brother Yataro's discovery of it, and his decision to fire into the air at the risk of his own life. At home, she reminded her children how William Penn had put up his fine sword, and quoted John Woolman's account of how committees of Quakers sat in Philadelphia and, while bloody victims of the Indian wars were carried through the streets, decided against paying taxes to carry on the wars.

She had told the children these stories before. But now the awakened minds of her family brought them to keen and painful life.

They spoke of the brotherhood of man and daringly mentioned Utopian schemes for communal living, only to learn that Shizu had thought all these things out before.

But it wasn't all one way. The young people attacked the forms of her religion and labeled as meaningless practices that seemed right and essential to Shizu. By now, too, they had found her own books, and read them back to her, even her favorite books about Elizabeth Fry.

"Listen to this," one of them would say mischievously, " 'The longer I live, the more difficult do I see education to be; more particularly as it regards the religious restraints we put upon our children . . . I begin seriously to doubt whether . . . it is not better quite to leave sober-minded young persons to judge for themselves.' " [1]

Shizu accepted their comments for the most part. She believed in the possibilities of youth and was as ready to learn from her children as she had been to teach them.

Chiyokichi wasn't standing still all this time, either.

[1] *Elizabeth Fry, Quaker Heroine,* by Janet Whitney. Boston, Little, Brown and Company, 1936. Used by permission.

He was working unceasingly to help one child after another make his way through college and out into the world. But no matter how hard he had to work, nor how fast the years sped by, his hearty love of life sought out ever new channels of enjoyment and fulfillment.

He took up the art of *bonsai* as a hobby. In the tree-fern purchased at the exposition he had planted some ordinary Monterey pine seeds, picturing in his mind the miniature trees he would some day develop. The seeds rooted and grew. As soon as they got a good start, Chiyokichi cut back the tap-root and the main stem, and bound the tap-root with copper wire. Then confined to a small pot, the trees flourished, carefully tended, watered, fed, and given plenty of outdoor air and sunlight.

Chiyokichi's knowing fingers gently changed their line of growth, curved them into beauty, and bound them to keep them firm.

Shizu loved the little trees. She planted some herself, and shared her outdoor time between them and her aviary of canaries. Chiyokichi began to send for seeds from Hokkaido, and from Nikko, where stands the temple-tomb of Ieyasu, made familiar to the children by Chiyokichi's story-telling. Now the family could look at miniature offspring of the very trees that sheltered the magnificent historic shrine. The little trees were not the sort of thing to make the fairy tales seem more real, however. Instead they moved Japan even farther beyond the understanding of the Takahashi children.

To the parents, Japan was also very far away. The

moment when they ceased entirely to imagine going back to live there had passed unnoticed, a long time ago. Now their wistful hope was that some time they would be allowed to become naturalized American citizens.

Still they were interested in all they heard from Japan.

Chiyokichi's older friend, Asataro Miyamori, had gone on from eminence as a professor to fame as a translator. He was the country's greatest authority on Shakespeare, and Shizu remembered with pleasure the days when he first struggled with Joseph Cosand to perfect his understanding of Shakespearean thought and she had translated for both of them.

Several of Chiyokichi's brothers had been killed in the wars with China and with Russia, but the others had been doing very well, in medicine, business, and the law, and the youngest was now a well-known publisher in Tokyo.

Inazo Nitobe had become the first president of the Woman's Christian College of Tokyo, but his influence went beyond education. He was a peacemaker, and one of the world's great internationalists. It seemed to Shizu that he had spent his life opposing war pressures in Japan. She recalled her first years at Joseph Cosand's school when Nitobe's warnings against Japanese militarism seemed so incomprehensible to her. Now she greeted his appointment to the secretariat of the League of Nations with heartfelt happiness.

And there was Ume Tsuda, Shizu's fellow-pupil in her first year at the Girls' School, who had started a unique international, non-sectarian school—Tsuda College.

These people had made their mark in the world. Their lives weighed in the balance. Did it seem to Shizu that hers had not had quite the significance she had so confidently expected? The P.T.A., the W.C.T.U., the church—were they enough? She had planned to make her life blaze her convictions for the Lord.

Even now, if she could go to the university and study again. . . . But the doctor said, "no."

There was her asthma, and there was her blood pressure. Since the birth of one of the later children, her blood pressure had been very high. A horrid buzzing in the head, dizziness, and faintness had come to cloud her sunniest moments—when she was speaking, or interpreting, or in a lively discussion. It laid her low when she most wanted to be up and doing.

Now, when she might make bright her lamp, had she run out of oil? I mustn't kick against the pricks, Shizu told herself; there is still work for me to do that is within my power.

And there was work, sad work.

September 1, 1923, Tokyo was struck by a terrific earthquake, followed by tidal waves and that most devastating of the "great catfish's" allies—fire.

Shizu learned of the destruction of her uncle's home, with all the precious family belongings she had hoped some day to repossess. The southern part of the city, however, where the Friends Mission Compound was, had been spared. The Friends were free to help the stricken, and Christian hands and hearts all over the world, including Shizu's, were active in behalf of the suffering.

It wasn't only in Japan that things were bad. America was suffering from an earthquake of the spirit. Hard times, lawlessness, the breakdown of prohibition inflamed the ugly moods of the country. Racial ill will grew, minorities suffered, and Oriental-hating groups took advantage of the times to push their case in Congress.

By the time informed and liberal groups were aroused, the Oriental Exclusion Law of 1924 had passed to become a part of national policy. Years later echoes of this unhappy action thundered at Pearl Harbor.

It was in this same dark year that personal grief came to the Takahashis. One evening they sat enjoying their garden and their birds, while the younger children played around them. The ball was thrown to Anna; she missed, and ran out in the street to get it.

She didn't see the car speeding toward her, and it was twilight—the driver didn't see her, either.

Now Shizu and Chiyokichi must search with blinded eyes for what consolation life and religion had stored up for them.

CHAPTER TEN

Landscape in Miniature

After Anna died, the house on Haste Street never seemed the same. Shizu kept telling herself it was the same. The history of the whole of the family's life could be read there, as the history of a tree could be seen in its rings. The improvements Chiyokichi had made, with such ingenuity and effort; the remodeling of the church into a dormitory; the remodeling of the dormitory into apartments; each additional room that had housed the growing family. The shop, the hothouse, the building now used by the Japanese Association, and above all, the garden. So many anxious hours, toilsome hours, and hours of satisfaction and pride were there recorded.

But for the moment the meaning had gone out of them. All the anxiety and toil and satisfaction had been in terms of what it meant to the children. Now that one of them was gone—even though so many were still around, troublesome and lovable as ever—the spirits of the parents seemed to flag.

They decided to move. This idea had been discussed before from time to time, but now objections to it seemed to have vanished. There was a search, complicated of course by the fact that they were not welcome everywhere. Finally a house was found on Carleton Street.

"It's quite a big house," Shizu said, coming in weary from the finally successful search, and sitting down at the dinner table to eat the meal the girls had put together.

A big house! What fun. Ernie tore off on his bicycle at the first opportunity to take a look. No one had told him the address, but he knew it was in the sixteen-hundred block, so he rode up and down until he saw an empty one. Big! It was enormous. Ernie felt that, living in that house, he would be kingpin of the neighborhood.

They moved. Ernie was eager on the front seat, leaning out of the window on the wind like a fox terrier.

"All right, here it is, here we are. Why don't you stop?" he directed.

"Because that is not the house," said his father, driving on a bit. "Here is our house."

Ernie sat back in the seat and stared at the low brown house. Well! That wasn't such a big house! What a gyp.

But when they went in and looked around, he found it was a good-sized house, after all, rambling back through large living room, dining room, and pantry to a generous garden space beyond. There was a large side yard, too.

Perhaps it was really this that Chiyokichi had bought —a place for gardening. After the move he did a little tailoring in a shop in San Francisco, but his eyes, used so exactingly and long, were giving out. His avocation now could move into the main part of his life. He began the landscaping of his space at once, built a cage for Shizu's prize canaries, and a little pool for golden carp. He set up tables on which to place his growing number of dwarf trees.

The children went on studying and being graduated with fine records from high school and college. In one year, 1932, three of them took degrees from the University of California: William, his Ph.D.; Michi, her degree in nursing; and Chiye, her degree in optometry.

Ai went to the Pacific School of Religion for graduate work, Yaye took a liberal arts course, looking toward social service, and Nobu also took a degree in optometry. George and Henry had established themselves as optometrists by this time.

"Say, this little garden is really cute," Henry said one day, picking up a wooden box in which a lovely landscape lived in miniature. There was a small tree, twisted with careful art to make a formal composition, with cones tiny as currants, and under it a clump of Chinese herb grass. One might wish, looking at it, that he could nibble one of Alice in Wonderland's magic cakes and walk around on the grass and rest under the tree.

"How about my taking it to the office and putting it in my window?" Henry asked. "I think people would like to see it."

Chiyokichi didn't mind. "It might draw attention to your work," he agreed.

And it did. It also drew attention to itself. Many people came in to ask about it. "Is it for sale? Well, could I order one like it?"

Henry sold two hundred and fifty of the little gardens during the next few years. They came to be well-known, and were exhibited in many places, at the Berkeley Congregational Church, the Friends Church, and the Y.W.C.A.

The little trees found an acceptance not always granted the grower. It was strange, this Janus-face of California life—or was it human nature? One face smiled at the little trees, or at babies of whatever complexion, or at an isolated person of foreign background; but the other frowned implacably at any group with differing characteristics.

News from Japan was not helpful to her former nationals and their children. Shizu had been gratified by much of the news from Japan in the early years. The new Emperor, Hirohito, had a modern education and liberal tendencies. Progressive ferment stirred the people. Manhood suffrage was made law. Changes seemed to give promise of permanence.

Shizu's satisfaction gradually changed to worried indignation. The liberals lost power in the disillusion that followed the first world war. Conservative Japanese army and navy officers gained strength in the government and rallied popular support with outcries against the Oriental Exclusion Act of 1924. Liberalism, internationalism, and democratic ideas had not established permanent roots among a people conditioned by ancient feudal customs. But national self-interest, nationalism, was a symbol understood by all.

"Look here!" Shizu would cry out from behind the morning paper. And then read the scare headline dramatically. "They've annexed Manchuria!"

"It's population pressure," one of her children would answer. "Do you realize the population over there nearly quadrupled in the last hundred years? From about twenty-six million to eighty million. What are they going to do with all those people?"

"Well, they shouldn't steal somebody else's country," Shizu said roundly.

"What else did the democracies do? Just take a look at England!"

"Well, the United States has never done it!"

"Why should we; look at all this space! Then think of Japan. Only as big as Montana in the first place, and practically all volcanoes at that."

"It doesn't matter. It isn't right."

In spite of Shizu's feelings, Manchuria became a puppet state, and in Japan even those who had opposed the adventure couldn't help seeing the glory and promise of their expanding empire. Some of the liberals still spoke out; Prince Saionji was one, but he was old and had to turn over his premiership to Prince Konoye, who reluctantly gave way to the pressure upon him.

Inazo Nitobe continued courageously to oppose the prevailing imperialist spirit. He never changed his views. In 1933 he was appointed delegate to the Pan-Pacific Conference, held that year in Banff, Canada. Here he spoke out for the last time—far-seeing, high-minded Christian statesman that he was. He died on the way home.

Despite his unpopular views, he had held the respect of his countrymen. General Sadao Araki, the same who had been whipping up anti-foreign feeling and imperialist ambition, said in 1934 to Kotoko Nitobe: "Are you the daughter of Dr. Inazo Nitobe? Ah, how great a loss! We need Dr. Nitobe in Japan now." [1]

In 1936, Shizu had many occasions for lament.

"They've murdered Korekiyo Takahashi!"

"Well, he's no relative," said Chiyokichi, and received an icy stare. "I know, he was a great Minister of Finance," he added hastily. Despite his lightness, Chiyokichi shared his wife's concern at the trend of events.

This Takahashi had been one of Japan's outstanding liberals. One of the early explorers of the outside world, he had worked as a domestic in America, and returned to rise to a position of universal respect. He, along with several other liberal statesmen, was murdered by a group of young officers.

Though the officers were punished, they had eliminated powerful opposition, and gained a reputation for decisive action. They decided they could go ahead with their plans.

"They've seized Peiping and Tientsin!" Shizu announced a little later.

Japan overran large parts of northern China; fought around Shanghai; took Nanking, and went on to Han-

[1] Related by Gurney Binford.

kow. Stories of the depredations in Nanking reached Shizu, and her sorrow was extreme.

"They didn't act that way before," she repeated. "I remember how it was during the Russo-Japanese War. What was it Count Oyama said? He made a proclamation—perhaps it was put up on that great billboard by the Nihonbashi, the main bridge in Tokyo. It was something about confining belligerent actions to the actual engagements, and there being no reason at all for enmity between individuals because their countries were at war. No, I can't believe the Nanking tales."

One of her daughters remonstrated gently, "I know atrocity stories in times of war should be taken with a gain of salt. But isn't it possible that Japanese soldiers who are so controlled—or one should better say repressed—at home, might break loose abnormally in war time, in a strange land? The very fact that in their own country everything is done in just a certain way with no room for initiative or using your own judgment might cause people to go berserk in an unaccustomed situation, and especially a terrible situation like war."

"Yes—war, war, it brings out the worst in people," Shizu agreed, tortured by sorrow and concern. "The end can never justify the means. He who takes the sword shall perish by the sword—either physically or morally."

The Japanese war in China reached a stalemate. The invaders settled on the countryside to await surrender by the Chinese Nationalists. In the meantime, dramatic events turned the eyes of the United States to the other direction. Hitler marched into Poland, and Great Britain declared war. In the United States, more men were conscripted for the Armed Services.

In the midst of all this, San Francisco for a time forgot its apprehension about world events in a happy preoccupation of her own. The Golden Gate International Exposition opened, and again all roads converged on the great beautiful bay.

This time there was no question as to what concession Chiyokichi would have; his exhibition of little trees and gardens won instant entrance to the Hall of Flowers.

Again the city teemed with visitors, and the treasures of the world were to be seen in a day's stroll. Again the Takahashi family had a chance to be a functioning part of the great enterprise, to meet all kinds of people, and enjoy new experiences. One they most enjoyed was a Japanese wrestler.

He found his way to the Hall of Flowers in the opening days, and after that spent most of his free time with the family. He was not at the exposition to wrestle, for he had retired and become the owner of a famous restaurant in Tokyo. He was a wonderful cook, and this was the art he was practicing at the exposition. He also cooked in the Takahashi home, bringing crabs from Fisherman's Wharf, rolling them in batter, and frying them to brown, crispy lightness—*tempura* of such delicate crustiness as even Chiyokichi could not achieve.

After dinner he and Chiyokichi would vie with one another in telling tales. They told about the wrestling tournaments and the excited crowds that thronged the matches. The wrestler described the Kokugikwan, the National Game Building.

"I can't believe it would be as exciting in a building as it used to be out-of-doors," Chiyokichi frequently exclaimed.

"Oh, believe me, it's more comfortable to be indoors, warm in January, and dry in June," the wrestler would answer, roaring with laughter at Chiyokichi's nostalgic and oft-repeated words.

Then he would push back his chair and tell them, perhaps, the story of Tanikaze, the beloved great wrestler of the past.

"Three hundred and sixty-five pounds, he weighed, before he hit his peak. He won a hundred and eighty-three out of two hundred and twenty matches. One match, he lost deliberately. It was to a poor wrestler who wasn't very skilled but who was devoted to his father. Tanikaze let him win the huge prize, so he could buy a shop for his father."

It was exciting, but strenuous, too. Next door to Chiyokichi's exhibit was the concession of the Trailways Bus Company. When he became overtired, he would slip away for a surreptitious nap in one of the big luxurious buses on display. Visitors marveled at the impressive vehicle, never suspecting that a small Japanese gentleman with a goatee was slumbering peacefully inside the cavernous depths.

He was awake, however, at the proper times, and he kept his tiny gardens in peak condition. When the time came for judging, his exhibit won first prize. In fact, his were the only Japanese plants that survived the chill of Treasure Island during the fall and winter months.

In 1940, his dwarf pines were displayed at the hobby show in "Playland." People were delighted with them, and bought, and placed orders, so that his business thrived and his prowess became well known.

"Something's wrong," he said one day to Shizu.

Shizu's face assumed an anxious expression. "Are you ill? Have you a pain somewhere? Oh, tell me quickly, what has happened."

"I have suffered a terrible loss," said Chiyokichi gravely, waiting momentarily for her reaction. "I have no more debts."

This was the time of harvest, and the parents enjoyed it. The children married, one by one, and the happy time of grandchildren arrived. George's wife, Yoshie, was a third-generation Christian, whose mother had taught in a Methodist Mission School in Japan. Yoshie had herself, after graduation from the University of California, gone back to Japan to teach for three years. William married a fine girl who had been his fellow-worker in the Young People's Christian Conference; Henry married a very beautiful girl whose concern for others had led her into becoming a nurse.

Shizu had news for her husband one day.

"I will tell you something important," she said, taking time to be a little tantalizing. "You have won many prizes and the children have earned honors and degrees. Now poor Shizu is to have an honor, too. I am to be a Mother of the Year, and I will be honored at a banquet of the University Mother's Club! It's almost as good as a degree! I will sit next to President Sproul, too."

"You will enjoy that," said Chiyokichi, "and you deserve it. Nine children graduated from the university! You have made a real contribution."

"*We* have made it," Shizu answered proudly.

CHAPTER ELEVEN

Let's Go Home

December 7, 1941. Shizu had been to church. Chiyokichi had stayed home and cooked dinner, and appetizing smells greeted Shizu and the children as they came in the house. While they were still eating, David, who loved music, turned on the radio to get a favorite concert.

Instead they heard the news of Pearl Harbor.

The family was stunned. They shared the same silent horror that listeners all over America experienced as they listened to the staccato news announcements.

"It must be Orson Welles again."

Someone turned the dial, and a new voice filled the room with grim reports.

"It's impossible."

"Japan wouldn't try such a crazy thing."

"They're still negotiating in Washington."

The voices faded away and the family grew silent as the radio blared forth the relentless details of disaster.

"They think America's too soft to make a real fight."

"It's crazy when you realize Japan's limitations."

"*Yamato tamashii!* The spirit of the Japanese. They believe they're invincible."

Confusion, incipient fear—a sense of unreality. Each family member sitting around the Takahashi table was absorbed in his own thoughts. The children torn by feel-ings of resentment and irritation while Shizu and Chi-yokichi, perhaps, pondered their alien status with a new concern.

Forty years of hard work in the United States, giving it the best they had. Forty years of working in the church, the school, the home, W.C.T.U., P.T.A. Forty years of integrity and unselfishness—yet it hadn't been enough to earn them the right to be naturalized. And now—

At evening service the people in the church were friendly—almost too friendly. They seemed to say, "Don't worry, you had nothing to do with it. We're back of you."

Somehow, even this was a shock. To think they'd need to say it. To think the fact of Pearl Harbor could reach out and draw a line between fellow-Christians so quickly.

Physically, the line was certainly there. What had been the Takahashi bank account became alien funds, and the parents had to borrow working capital from their children. Grocers refused to wait on them, and milkmen to deliver. One day Shizu came home quite breathless with indignation from a meeting where a Christian speaker had anathematized all Japanese—a speaker who should have known the facts, been able to use judgment, and discuss the tragedy with under-standing. Instead, Shizu had felt herself thrust into the same category with feudal-minded Japanese militarists, and heard the door slammed on her and the key turned gratingly in the lock.

Several issei well-known to the Takahashis were visited by the F.B.I. and taken away for questioning.

"How could they suspect Mr. Saito of anything?"

"He taught in a language school one year, remem-ber?"

"As if that meant anything! And Mr. Ozaka?"

"He went to Japan last year—that must be the reason. He went to visit his old mother."

Shizu read the papers now with agonized intensity.

She was encouraged when Attorney General Biddle warned against the persecution of enemy aliens, but soon came the rumor that all enemy aliens would be removed from the state.

She read in the paper unbelievable accounts of sub-version by resident Japanese and on the other hand exaggerated stories of violence against them. (Actually, according to official Government reports, there never was sabotage either on the West Coast or in Hawaii, not a single case involving issei or nisei.)

Reputable papers took up the hate campaign begun so many years ago in the *Sacramento Bee*. Editorials, letters to the editor—their venom increased from day to day. Soon the public clamor for removal of Japanese residents from the West Coast drowned out the voices raised in their support.

On February 13, there came the announcement that struck Shizu to the heart. The Wallgren Committee, made up of West Coast Congressmen, recommended to the President that all Japanese, both aliens and citizens, be evacuated.

The children, too! Her children, to whom she and Chiyokichi had given the gift of American citizenship! What sort of gift had it turned out to be?

The weeks and months ahead were marked by chaotic confusion for the Takahashis and their friends, due in part to the confusion in regulations and directives issued by the Federal Government, as authority was shifted from the Justice Department to the Western Defense Command. Japanese families—citizens and aliens alike —were removed from one area only to be moved again to another. There was a period of voluntary evacuation. Finally total removal to specially constructed camps was ordered.

The Takahashis, in preparing for departure, were considerably more fortunate than most. Shizu, who had not submitted to segregation of the spirit for one single day since her arrival in America, had formed a broad base of friends and understanding. Chiyokichi had achieved wide recognition with his miniature trees. They enjoyed financial security. They and their children were able to arrange without untold hardship for the necessary disposition of their homes, their businesses, and all but the few possessions that they were permitted to take along.

The great concerns of Shizu and Chiyokichi were

their trees and their canaries. They found renters who undertook to care for these, as part payment for their rent.

"Don't forget, they are alive," urged Chiyokichi, going from one to another of his beautiful little trees, clipping here, and touching the earth there to see if it was moist and soft. "They can't move, but they need care just as a child needs care. Feed them occasionally, and, please, don't let them thirst! Trim them twice a year, and they will be all right."

The day came when they must go. There was a kind of sad dignity about the occasion. The Japanese were calm in face, calmer than the people who came to give them coffee and doughnuts and say good-by. These were mostly church people, but usually they didn't know the exiles very well. Even though perhaps a third of the Japanese who were evacuated were Christians, they had never been urged to mingle with Caucasian Christians. As trains and buses moved away, the faces at the windows tried to smile to hide their fears.

It was a moment of stark tragedy not only for the passengers, two thirds of whom were American citizens, but for the nation. Justice Frank Murphy characterized the evacuation as the "legalization of racism" during a later Supreme Court hearing, and students of democracy and civil liberties have been concerned at the precedent that was established when the buses and trains started their long journey.

O Lord, I am a stranger on the earth, hide not thy face from me, thought Shizu, as she gazed at the soldiers with fixed bayonets who guarded them. She tried to concentrate on George Fox, his trials; and the daunt, less mission journeys of his followers in the 1600s, when they traveled, men and women alike, far into the East in search (four hundred years too late) of Prester John, and received lashes and imprisonment. She thought back on Mary Fisher and Ann Austin, landing in Massa, chusetts, only to be robbed and imprisoned and shipped off to Barbados; of Elizabeth Dyer, who was hanged.

But when she tried to bolster up her courage with a feeling of common trials with the heroes of her faith, one thought always checked her: *they* did it for a reason; *they* had a purpose; *they* suffered for a cause.

The Takashashi parents and their younger children were taken to Tanforan, the assembly center hastily organized at a race track. Because of Shizu's asthma, acute after the dust of the journey, their family was assigned to the jockey's quarters instead of to a horse's stall, like most people.

This had its drawbacks. Preferential treatment natu, rally brought suspicion and resentment from other evac, uees, none of whom were in their most balanced and reasonable state of mind.

Shizu tried to maintain an encouraging point of view. When the children complained about a neighbor's hos, tility, or about the poor food served in the noisy mess hall, or the lack of privacy, or the everlasting Japanese, ness of everything, she said:

"Well, it won't be much longer. They say that in the relocation camps we will have nice places to live, and something to do. Work for everyone, with pay on the regular wage-scale, they say. We won't have to stay long there, either, I'm sure of it."

She tried to believe it, and she tried not to worry about the married children, who, living in different evacuation zones, had been taken to other camps. Through long, pain-filled nights she stayed awake and tried not to worry, for her habitual insomnia was worse. In fact, she was not well at all.

By the time they got to Poston, Shizu could no longer cheer the others up, and they all turned to, in every effort to make things easier for her. No one pointed out that the "nice places to live" were rows and rows of hundred-foot barracks, four to six families in each. They didn't speak of the dust that blew across the desert, through the clusters of barracks, and covered every surface, indoors and out, with a gritty film. They didn't mention that the idea of work for everyone had been abandoned, that jobs had dwindled to a few low-echelon clerical and teaching jobs not already claimed by Caucasians. Nor did they say too much about the "pay on the regular wage-scale," which had turned out to be twelve, sixteen, or nineteen dollars a month. All the children but young David managed to find something to do. Chiye taught flower arrangement, Yaye taught sewing; Joe was assistant teacher in the third and fourth grades.

Chiyokichi was good-natured and lively, making friends and telling stories, making fun out of discomfort. When there was trouble, such as did boil up now and then between issei and nisei, especially in the more restricted far-west camps like Poston, they didn't discuss it much.

They never spoke of the fence—nor the sentries.

Shizu's illness became acute, and necessitated an operation. She almost felt like giving up.

Her children, here, in *prison*—for she knew about the fence. She wasn't able to go out and see it, but she felt its choking confinement. Everyone felt it. They had not resisted the evacuation—why a fence? They had acquiesced in the judgment of their government, and continued their habit of being law-abiding citizens—to what avail? To be insulted by a fence, a high, barbed-wire enclosure.

Was this what she and Chiyokichi had come to America for? Was this the end of his adventure, and her pilgrimage?

In her distress she called upon the Lord, and cried to her God.

The operation was successful, and Shizu rallied well. She began to get stronger, and in the resurgence of health, something happened to her. Now she was able to read again, her Bible and her well-worn volumes of Friends' writings, and somehow she found things she hadn't found before.

"Listen to this. John Woolman, talking of slavery: 'I believe He who is a refuge for the oppressed will, in His own time, plead their cause, and happy will it be for such as walk in uprightness before Him.' "

One of her daughters answered slowly, "That's what

you always told us. 'To walk in uprightness,' as he puts it, is what matters, and what happens to us doesn't really matter. But it's kind of hard to really believe it."

"And then there's this one," Shizu added eagerly. " 'Traveling up and down of late, I have had renewed evidences that to be faithful to the Lord, and content with his will concerning me, is a most necessary and useful lesson for me to be learning; looking less at the effects of my labor than at the pure motion and reality of the concern, as it arises from heavenly love.' " [1]

Shizu sat silent, as though alone, looking straight ahead. As it had happened several other times in her life, there came into her mind an illumination that almost physically warmed her. Here, on another mountain trail, the steepest one of all, suddenly rose the sun.

There had been, all through evacuation and relocation, something that might be called a trickle of Christian love coming to the exiles in the camps. Cups of coffee and sandwiches and doughnuts. Boxes of crayons, sometimes used and broken. Dog-eared books. Useful supplies. Letters. Visits from churches near the camps, and where possible, invitations to the evacuees to visit in churches and homes nearby.

It all counted. Church groups sent regular representatives to the camps to visit the people, any people who needed them. They appealed cases of injustice where evacuees had been misled into incriminating replies when questioned about loyalty, and they went to bat

[1] *The Journal of John Woolman*, ed. by Janet Whitney. Chicago, Henry Regnery Co., 1950. Used by permission.

for the "potentially dangerous" who had been picked up by the F.B.I. and interned in prison camps. They tried to protect the remaining property of the evacuees (90 per cent had by now lost some or all of their property). They lobbied for release of the evacuees and set up hostels, to be ready when people would be permitted to leave camp. They arranged scholarships all over the country for young citizens when they were free again, and enlisted aid wherever possible for jobs and training opportunities.

Shizu, well-known and well-beloved, received many visitors. One was Herbert Nicholson, who with his wife Madeline, had been associated with church work near Tokyo for many years. Now both were working tirelessly among the evacuees.

Mr. Nicholson assured Shizu that plans for the release of the evacuees were progressing.

"I'm sure we can get you out pretty soon, with your family," he said to Shizu. "With your health, and with the fact that everybody knows you. They've announced that twenty-five thousand can be released this year."

"Of course, it's hard to know just where to go. Most of the Western states—all but Colorado, I guess—are trying to imitate California's 'hospitality.' They won't have a thing to do with us."

"Never mind, we can find places in the Middle West. Things are getting better. Nisei can volunteer now, you know."

"Yes—for a special combat team. Why can't they just join up like anybody else?"

Many of the nisei wondered that. But actually, the saga of the 442nd Infantry Combat Team turned out to be a dramatic vindication of the nisei. Their record was exceptional, their courage was phenomenal. Indeed, they became the army's most decorated unit, and the number of their "purple hearts" was more than double the strength of the team. But in an Oregon town, sixteen dead nisei were removed from the Honor Roll, and ads were run in the paper suggesting that the Japanese Americans sell their land, as no one wanted them back.

The Takahashis were among the first to leave Poston. Father, Mother, Chiye, Yaye, and Joe went to Chicago. David, the youngest, went to Oberlin College and later into the Armed Services, and Michi went to Madison to a nursing position. Before long, other members of the family joined the parents. They found a vast old house where they all could live.

"What a relief to be together again!" Shizu murmured, glorying in their presence.

But in a family like theirs, just being together was not enough. Each small group needed a spot of its own; each of Shizu's children needed a place to fill, a piece of work to do.

Henry got a job with the United States Treasury Department. William continued his research in plant viruses and his discoveries were of great aid to the army in the tropics. In 1945 he won a Guggenheim Fellowship. Ernest became Dean of the Monroe College of Optometry. Chiye, who had never really liked being an optometrist and whose skillful fingers preferred to sketch, design, or arrange flowers, went to the Chicago Art Institute and later took a good designing position. All found places and made their way with ease in the big, cold gray city which was so objectively friendly.

"It's almost a shock to be able to rent a house so easily —after you find one, of course. Just as if Grandpa'd been a viking or a padrone, instead of a samurai!"

"And have you noticed, there's a Baptist church downtown with a nisei pastor and as diverse a congregation as you could hope to find."

"Well, I never thought we felt discrimination very much—on account of Mother and all. But somehow I guess I must have been sort of braced against it, anyway. I get the oddest feeling here that I must be invisible or something when they look at me, and their eyes don't say 'Japanese.' "

Shizu still read the newspapers. In January, 1945, she read that the Japanese were permitted to return to California.

"Oh, how will they be treated?" she cried to Chiyokichi. "Will it be like before?"

Chiyokichi made a gesture of seasoned skepticism. There was no bitterness in it, just a recognition of the long, long way humanity had to go before it became even reasonable.

During the first half of the year there were thirty cases of ill-treatment on a large scale for Shizu to read about in her paper.

The Takahashis also heard from friends that their own affairs had been, not sabotaged, but neglected. The first renters of their home had moved away; those who moved in had been indifferent to their obligations, and neglected the garden and the little trees.

"Some of the maples," wrote a friend, "have grown to as much as five feet."

"Well, what shall we do?" asked Chiyokichi. "The children are getting restless here. We must decide where we want to be, whether to go or stay. Which shall it be? You know what may be waiting for us if we do go back. Unfriendliness is the least of it; it may be even bodily harm."

"I don't believe it!" Shizu cried out strongly. "I think the hate is dying down. I think the church people are working hard to change things. I believe it's going to be different now. People are really good inside, and they have learned a lot!"

She thought back over the years of exile. She, at least, had learned a lot. "To be faithful to the Lord and content with his will concerning me."

Shizu said what so many other Americans of Japanese birth or background were also saying, all over the eastern part of the country. She didn't say, "I believe I'll go back there to that place from which I was driven out." She didn't say "I think I'll give the people another chance to prove they're human, even Christian."

She only said, "Let's go home."

Epilogue

My family and I drove clear across the country in 1956 to see the Takahashis. Our mutual friends, Mr. and Mrs. Harry S. Nako, and their pastor, Rev. R. Dean Short, had introduced us to the Takahashis at a distance, and our interest in Shizu's life was great enough to compel the visit, even though Shizu herself had gone on before.

We drove up to the house that Ernie had been so disappointed in, and recognized it without needing the address, for it's embowered in lovely greenery.

A little boy ran out as soon as we had stopped.

"How do you do; I'm Joel," he announced.

We introduced ourselves.

"How are you, Mr. and Mrs. Hull? How are you, children?" he continued. "Your station wagon's very dirty."

"We haven't had a chance to get it cleaned. Why don't you wash it for us?" suggested my husband jovially.

"All right! I will!" Joel ran into the house, crying,

"Pans of water, Mother, and cloths! I'm going to wash a station wagon!"

We had a time dissuading him, and this broke the ice, if there ever could have been any ice in this friendly family. The house was full of friendliness, and little boys' things, and from the wall portraits of Shizu and Chiyokichi looked down at us. They had been painted from photographs taken by Henry, a talented amateur photographer.

We were able to look from Mr. Takahashi on the wall, benign and dignified in his kimono, to Mr. Takahashi in the flesh, welcoming and interested. But Shizu we must remember through her children, while her pictured face looked down on us, serious, determined, and lovable.

They showed us the garden—the pool, the shrubs, and the little trees, which were even more beautiful than we had imagined from hearing of them. They showed us Shizu's canaries in their big aviary.

"Papa thought of letting them fly after the funeral," said Yaye. "It was a symbol, to him. But then he was afraid something would happen to them, since they were only used to the cage."

They gave us dinner, chicken teriyaki and all kinds of good, though more accustomed foods, like spaghetti, and cherry tarts, and cream puffs.

Then afterward we gathered round the dining table to talk about their mother. Mr. Takahashi was a little too tired to join the group. But eight of his living children were there, (young David had died before finishing

his university course) with a good many of their husbands or wives, and children coming in and out.

"Do you remember?" was the refrain, and leaning forward each would tell a part, while his face brimmed with
warm amusement and love.

"Do you remember how Mother used to enter con-
tests? There was one for a slogan, and she won five
dollars. What was it? 'Treat your friends with—some
kind of coffee.'"

"Wasn't it 'Keep your friends—with that kind of
coffee?'"

"Anyway, she won it. Remember that contest where
you were given a girl's name at the drug store with every
fifty-cent purchase, and then if you had the name they
drew there was a prize? When the winning name was
announced, it was Henrietta—we had had it, but it was
lost! How Mother scoured the house for it! We never
found it, though."

"She was so interested in everything. Especially about
the university. When they had boat races she got so excited, but she never could say 'regatta' just right, or
'Poughkeepsie.'"

"Never stopped trying, though. And you're right
about the university. I'm sure she never gave up hope
of going there and getting a degree."

They told about their father's trip to Japan in 1948.
He flew in! This was the big thrill for the village that
he'd left when he was thirteen. People lined the streets
to greet him, and he invited everyone over sixty years
to a banquet. He sat at the head of the table with his

publisher brother, and was kept busy receiving the congratulations and questions of his friends. They were sure he must know everything, but once in a while he had to have a consultation with his brother!

They told about a later trip he'd made. This time he took Chiye, in order that she could perfect her artistry in flower arrangement. She was already so accomplished that she was admitted to a special seminar of sixty experts, where the particular styles and colors to be stressed for the coming year are determined. The trip was of great joy and value to her.

To Chiyokichi it was something like a pilgrimage. He went back to the Friends Mission Compound, visited the new school buildings, and then went to the meetinghouse. It was a new meetinghouse, and over the fireplace in the office was a memorial photograph of Shizu Higuchi Takahashi.

While we talked, Joel had come rushing through the room periodically with his cousin Janet, Ernie's little girl. On one of the many trips, he was carrying the telephone book.

He stopped to give us his attention. "Look here," he said, holding up the enormous book. "See all these names! I'll read some of them to you. Nelson, Walter; Nelson, Walter C.; Nelson, Walter M.; Nelson, Wanda—"

"Oh, Joel," said his mother. "Don't read any more just now. He reads it all the time," she explained to us. 'It seems to fascinate him."

But Joel was not to be put off his favorite subject.

He sat down to pursue it seriously, with the big book in his small, five-year-old lap.

"Do you know," he announced portentously, "that they have one of these books at the post office? I saw it there the other day. And—" now he was confidential, bursting with his thrilling news. "My mother tells me everybody has one! Just the same as us!"

His whole intelligent little face beamed at this revelation of the unity of mankind.

How like your grandmother, I thought. And there is just a chance, little Joel, that you won't have to keep your faith against such heavy odds.

Pronunciation Guide

Japanese syllables are short, consisting of a vowel and a single or double consonant, and are unstressed. Consonants are generally pronounced as in English; vowels are pronounced as follows:

A to rhyme with Ma
E to rhyme with May
I to rhyme with Me
O to rhyme with Oh
U to rhyme with Moo

Example: Shizuko, pronounced she-zoo-koh.

Glossary

bonsai	miniature tree
chin-chin-chiro-rin	the chirping sound of a cricket
daimyo	feudal lord
go-chiso	a feast
gomen kudasai	pardon me
goningumi	five-household group of peasants (Tokugawa)

haiku	seventeen syllable poem
hotokesama	souls of the dead (Buddhist)
inari	harvest god, a fox (Shinto)
issei	Japanese immigrant
kabuki	a highly stylized drama form using music and dance
kokutai	Japanese national feeling
namazu	legendary catfish that is said to cause earthquakes
niisan	eldest brother
nisei	a native born American of Japanese parentage
oban	Buddhist memorial festival of recollection
o-kai	rice gruel
obi	sash that binds the kimono
saké	rice wine
samurai	military class of feudal Japan; a knight
san	an honorific form attached to proper nouns
sensei	teacher
seppuku	ceremonial suicide
shoji	sliding wooden-framed panels of translucent paper; used as doors or to divide a room
Tokugawa	a powerful family that exercised control in Japan for almost two hundred years and gave their name to the historical period of seclusion
wakarimasen	I don't understand
Yamato tamashii	unconquerable spirit of the Japanese

The text of this book was set in 12 point Kentonian leaded 2 points, combined with two styles of Bernhard for the display type. The complete book was manufactured in New York by Book Craftsmen Associates.

TYPOGRAPHIC DESIGN BY DOROTHY PAPY
BINDING BY LOUISE E. JEFFERSON

Yet there was much that was good, too. There was the church to which Shizu led her family with confidence that they would not be rebuffed and which did not disappoint her. There were Chiyokichi's shrewdness and artistry that led him at last into a profitable business. There were the abundant gifts of the children that could not be hidden. There was the glorious day when Shizu's years of sacrifice were crowned with honor—she was chosen "mother of the year"!

There was, however, one last Gethsemane to be endured. World War II came, and with it the family's removal to a relocation camp. It was hard not to be bitter, but faith and time had completed the family's philosophy — ". . . to be faithful to the Lord and content." When the war ended and restrictions were removed, Shizu said simply, "Let's go home."

This is a story that will both shame and inspire the reader. It is a moving chronicle of the human spirit.

THE ARTIST

Miné Okubo is a versatile artist who has illustrated for leading magazines and newspapers, has been exhibited widely both at home and abroad, and has won several awards. She was a lecturer in art at the University of California for two years. Miss Okubo is at present living in New York City and devoting a major part of her time to creative painting. She has illustrated several books for Friendship Press.

Mr. and Mrs. Takahashi, whose story is told in *Suddenly the Sun*

Eleanor Hull, biographer of Shizu and Chiyokichi Takahashi and their children, has enough energy and enthusiasm for all of her varied interests. As the wife of a busy minister in Cleveland and mistress of a parsonage that seems to overflow with her five energetic children, she has what most women would consider a full-time career. But Mrs. Hull has managed to keep her family interested and actively participating in her second career as an author.

When she became interested in doing research on the Takahashi family for the purpose of writing *Suddenly the Sun,* the entire Hull family hopped into a car and set out for California. At the end of their journey the young Hulls met the third generation Takahashis, and there was a warm interchange between the two American families. One notable result of the meeting may be seen in the living reality of the characters in the book.

Mrs. Hull has written several popular juveniles for Friendship Press. She is the daughter of another well-known writer, Florence Crannell Means.

Paper $1.50